T0342047

CORPORATE TURNAROUND ARTISTRY

Corporate

TURNAROUND ARTISTRY

Fix Any Business in 100 Days

JEFF SANDS, CTP

WILEY

Published by John Wiley & Sons, Inc., Hoboken, New Jersey.
Published simultaneously in Canada.

For general information on our other products and services or for technical support, please contact our Customer Care Department within the United States at (800) 762-2974, outside the United States at (317) 572-3993, or fax (317) 572-4002.

Wiley publishes in a variety of print and electronic formats and by print-on-demand. Some material included with standard print versions of this book may not be included in e-books or in print-on-demand. If this book refers to media such as a CD or DVD that is not included in the version you purchased, you may download this material at http://booksupport.wiley.com. For more information about Wiley products, visit www.wiley.com.

Library of Congress Cataloging-in-Publication Data

Names: Sands, Jeff, author.
Title: Corporate turnaround artistry : fix any business in 100 days / Jeff Sands.
Description: Hoboken, New Jersey : Wiley, [2020] | Includes bibliographical references and index.
Identifiers: LCCN 2019052151 (print) | LCCN 2019052152 (ebook) | ISBN 9781119539988 (hardback) | ISBN 9781119540007 (adobe pdf) | ISBN 9781119539995 (epub)
Subjects: LCSH: Corporate turnarounds.
Classification: LCC HD58.8 .S2595 2020 (print) | LCC HD58.8 (ebook) | DDC 658.4/063—dc23
LC record available at https://lccn.loc.gov/2019052151
LC ebook record available at https://lccn.loc.gov/2019052152

Cover Design: Wiley
Cover Image: © zhudifeng/iStock.com

Printed in the United States of America

10 9 8 7 6 5 4 3 2 1

I've won life's lottery in family, and friends. I love each of you and am forever grateful for your gifts. Especially you, Alex – you're amazing.

To all the capitalists who serve humanity. May we have the courage to ensure that capitalism continues to serve humanity.

CONTENTS

ABOUT THE AUTHOR

J eff Sands is a corporate turnaround specialist who has devoted his career to saving businesses, jobs, and the communities they support. He grew up in a family manufacturing business and returned in his thirties to run, grow, fix, grow again, fix again, and eventually lose that business in the wake of Hurricane Katrina. Since then, Jeff has focused solely on saving other businesses and has developed a reputation as the best guy to call in the worst situations.

Jeff is a Certified Turnaround Practitioner (CTP) who was awarded a coveted TMA Turnaround of the Year Award in each of 2017, 2018, and 2019 and also the 2020 Turnaround Consultant of the Year by M&A Advisor. He consults select clients through Dorset Partners LLC (www.DorsetPartners .com) and pursues distressed industrial acquisitions through American Industrial Acquisition Corp. (www.AIAC.com).

He actively seeks distressed industrial acquisitions on a global basis and pays healthy finder fees for businesses with the following criteria:

- Peak revenues between $50 million and $500 million
- Broken income statement or balance sheet or both

- Liabilities assumed: environmental, pension, litigation, tax, etc.

- Seller reps and warranties: minimal

He is fully funded, can deliver a letter of intent in 7 days, and transact in under 30.

Jeff married his college sweetheart and they raised three wonderful and independent children. Despite being impatient and relentless, Jeff is the happiest guy on Earth.

FOREWORD

It's about time....

At some point in your business career you will own, or work for, do business with, buy from, sell to, finance, or advise a business in drastic need of a turnaround. With virtually similar certainty you will prove to be unprepared for such a challenge. It doesn't matter what college you graduated from or what company you rose within. You will lack knowledge of even the most rudimentary facets of how to deal with such a reality. In fact, you won't know where to turn for help ... until now. The business world needs this book, and Jeff Sands is uniquely qualified to deliver its message.

Perhaps your interest in business turnarounds is sparked by the hard reality that you presently find yourself engaged in one; or maybe you're impressively proactive and wish to forever avoid the need for one (bravo!); or maybe you wish to become a turnaround artist yourself. Happily, in these pages you will learn from someone who has played each of these roles. Not only will you learn the broad concepts of various approaches, but you can literally compile a to-do list for first-day activities, staff management, leadership, cash-preservation methods, strategy development, stake holder relations ... all of it. Best yet, these recommendations and the entertaining war stories that portray them, are offered up by someone who has been there, done that.

Although I am presently a professor of entrepreneurial practice at Syracuse University's Whitman School of Management, teaching has been a comparatively recent vocation. In the 20-plus years prior, I co-founded and built a commercial finance company from the ground up. I unexpectedly crossed paths with Jeff Sands while trying to find an acquirer for one of my client firms. My client had just notified me that their remaining corporate life expectancy was measured in just days. I didn't fancy having to don my executioner's outfit (initiating the process of shutting them down), and I personally liked the firm's owner. So I resolved to help find a solution. After networking with regional professionals for just half a day, the name Jeff Sands repeatedly arose. Like many, I knew that turnaround operators existed, but I knew little of this exotic practice or their methods.

With great speed and skill, Jeff engaged with my troubled client, conducted as much due diligence as could be readily completed, and within days had obtained a strong working knowledge of the problems facing this struggling company. With the agreement of my firm to forebear (a concept you'll soon learn more about) and my commitment to continue to provide funding, Jeff got to work. In the coming weeks and months, he achieved Herculean results by studiously following the very principles outlined in this book.

Some time later, after I entered academia, my administrators graciously encouraged me to create a course of my choosing. We quickly seized upon the topic of "Entrepreneurial Turnarounds." My premise was that many struggling enterprises could be successfully revived through the application of entrepreneurial principles. Surely, I thought, there must be many such business school courses around the country. As I began the task of laying out the curriculum, I quickly realized that (1) there are precious few university courses that focus on this topic anywhere in the world, (2) there is no publication or book designed as a text for such a course, and (3) in fact, there are hardly any publications anywhere that truly deliver the how-tos of turning a business around.

Undaunted, I immediately sought Jeff's opinions. He confirmed all my observations about the dearth of practical knowledge in this industry, and graciously agreed to assist me in course development. He sat for recorded interviews and provided supportive counsel throughout. Whether that experience helped form the genesis of this book, only its author knows. But I can tell you that this book stands alone among others on the industry bookshelf. Of course you can buy tomes written by famous industry titans that regale readers of their abundant wisdom as they embellish their exploits in their career's singular turnaround of a large company. Of interest is that these very same leaders were supported by legions of consultants and strategists, and they rarely dirtied their hands with the actual heavy lifting needed in a turnaround. Unfortunately, to glean practicable and implementable knowledge to create similar magic for your enterprise, you'd need to read dozens of such books.

Instead, Jeff Sands has written a how-to book with his sleeves rolled up and a decade of experience dripping from every fast-turning page. He takes real-world business concepts, some of them esoteric, and with a humorous flair, implants the seeds of knowledge throughout. Herewith an industry practitioner has written a book that delivers abundant education to everyone fortunate enough to turn its pages. You will come to realize that many businesses left to die could have enjoyed a better fate had their leaders proved smarter, or more aware of the task before them. Jeff correctly points out that the dearth of true instructional material on this topic is profound. In writing this book, he pulls back the curtain to enable readers to see the mechanics of how true turnaround professionals operate. In sharing his wisdom, we now have the chance to learn turnaround intricacies from a national-caliber, award-winning practitioner.

Regardless of the circumstance that has brought you to these pages, I promise you that this book and the knowledge it imparts will make you a better business person in innumerable ways. It may end up saving your business, enabling you to avoid future crisis, or developing a turnaround strategy "for a friend." It may even, as it does each year with my students, cause you to contemplate a career as a turnaround professional saving the jobs and careers of many.

Kenneth P. Walsleben
Professor of Entrepreneurial Practice
Whitman School of Management
Syracuse University

PREFACE

The ideal audience for this book is me 18 years ago: suddenly caught in a turnaround situation, confused as hell, banks calling the shots in their weird cryptic tones that I didn't understand, employees looking at me bug-eyed, silently pleading for leadership and a swarm of foreign pressures I never learned about in my MBA courses or the years of work life that had brought me to this place. By extension, this book is written for the entrepreneurs or CEOs who find themselves restless and unable to sleep at 2:00 a.m. trying to understand the world of insolvency, workouts, and turnarounds.

I'm hoping to contribute to the limited information that exists on the topic of corporate turnarounds. Ideally entrepreneurs would understand the downside of a business cycle before they wagered their home and their kid's college education on a new business venture. In my practice I've found the psychology of leaders dealing with stress and crisis to be one of the greatest influences on success and failure though I feel it has been greatly underdiscussed in the existing literature. Similarly, commercial debt restructuring lacks discussion in the literature out there.

Why artistry? Because turnarounds would be doomed to failure by the numbers. The businesses are out of cash and have been drained of value, and yet somehow a good turnaround artist can consistently win the game with this lousy poker hand. It's a game of speed, confidence, and building alliances.

Key Terms

The following terms are used frequently throughout this text.

Collateral The assets that back a loan. This is the car in your car loan, the house in your home mortgage.

CRO (chief restructuring officer) Similar to a turnaround consultant but with control. Some CROs may be actual employees and corporate officers, whereas others might be independent consultants filling that role.

Insolvency versus bankruptcy Insolvency is being broke and unable to pay your bills. Bankruptcy is a very specific legal process administered by the Federal Bankruptcy Court. Lay people use the word *bankruptcy* to mean broke or out of business, whereas I use it only in the strict legal definition.

Owner/entrepreneur/debtor/CEO I use these terms somewhat interchangeably to represent the individual dealing with financial distress. It is the lead person who is responsible for addressing these issues.

Secured creditors Usually your secured creditor is your bank, as well as lenders who have liened your assets and can foreclose on those assets in the event of a default. Secured creditors have the legal right to kill a business quickly, unsecured creditors cannot.

Unsecured creditors Generally vendors, people who are legitimately owed money but don't have liens filed against your assets (they can't foreclose on you).

Upside down This term usually refers to a balance sheet when liabilities are greater than the value of assets. It's another way of describing an insolvent balance sheet.

Zone of insolvency A somewhat nebulous zone when a company cannot foreseeably pay its current and future bills, or when the company's balance sheet has negative value (upside down). When a company slips into the zone of insolvency, the legal fiduciary obligation of corporate officers expands to include creditors in addition to shareholders and the corporation.

Disclaimer

All stories retold here are true, but details have been obscured to protect client confidentiality. Most stories are mine and I'm relaying firsthand experience. A few of the cases are repeats that I've heard from trusted friends, or perhaps an industry legend.

I am not an attorney. I am not offering legal advice. Consult a legal professional before you try any of this at home. Additionally, I am not a tax advisor and am not offering tax advice.

ACKNOWLEDGMENTS

Writing a book is a tremendous challenge and was made possible by the help of many friends and mentors. I wish to thank the Honorable Judge James Tancredi, Professor Ken Walsleben, Attorneys Peter Tamposi, Terry Kirwan, Joe Selinger, Kristin Wainwright, and Martin Nussbaum. Thanks also to my turnaround mentors and colleagues: Dave Sands, Van Lanier, Leonard Levie, Larry Small, Paul Fioravanti, Harrison Sangster, and Dave Cryer. And fellow authors: Bobby Guy, Mark Filippell, Drew Rozell, Jim Shein, Francis Ignatius Mortimer, Jonathan Friedland, James Sprayregen, and Carley Adler Nussbaum, each of whom provided invaluable guidance as I was trying to find my way through this endeavor.

Special thanks to my editor at Wiley, Sheck Cho, my project editor Elisha Benjamin, my production editor, Sharmila Srinivasan, copyeditor, Tami Trask, and proofreader, Michael Isralewitz.

Chapter 1

Understanding Corporate Turnarounds

If stupidity got us into this mess then why can't it
get us out?

—*Will Rogers*

The U.S. Federal Bankruptcy Court in New Orleans would never be described as regal or stately. Instead of marble floors and ornate molding it held all the charm of a Soviet era department of motor vehicle office: pale fluorescent lighting washed the stale air, dingy yellowing cinderblock walls sweated with the morning's dew. Metal chairs were lined up in orderly rows across the dead linoleum tile. A judge and her clerks worked behind two large wooden tables stacked high with files. It was just me and all the other losers assembled there that day to file personal Chapter 7 bankruptcy. I had a 780 credit score but that was about to tank because I'd personally guaranteed corporate debt on our family business prior to Hurricane Katrina and was now at rock bottom of society surrendering my assets to the court in exchange for a release of my debts.

Forty years of my life had led me to this low point. Our family home and neighborhood were wrecked in the storm, so my wife, our three young children, and I spent eight months living in a small camper in the driveway while we rebuilt the house on nights and weekends. My participation trophy was this day in court. I'd reached bottom and it was time to push off and rebuild, but I had few options; no corporation would hire a failed entrepreneur and I was dead broke without money to start or buy another business, and my credibility and confidence were both pretty well shot. Metaphorically I was naked and alone, picking myself up from the dust of my own failure. Every bone in my body yearned for security and comfort, and I dreamed of a cushy corporate job at a cushy company far away from the chaotic and punitive nature of insolvency. Well, almost every bone in my body yearned for that security and comfort, a small upset part of me wanted to stay right there in the dirt and fight my way back, which is ultimately what I did.

In those brief moments when my mind was not racing with anxiety, I reflected back … I'd played my cards wrong. I zigged when I should have zagged. The bank and its attorneys always seemed to know what was happening, but I rarely did. My corporate attorney didn't understand insolvency, whereas my bankruptcy attorney was a one-trick pony who only knew how to file bankruptcy. I'd been a checkers player trapped in a game of chess.

I'm a godawful loser, so I began to obsess about what could have been. I gave up hobbies and casual reading and churned through every book and article I could find on the topics of insolvency. I re-read all my college finance and account-ing textbooks and obsessively relived the last five years of my life which had led me to this gut-wrenching failure. I sought out corporate turnaround pros and befriended them. I talked my way into interviews with most of the major East Coast restructuring firms, I helped friends with their chal-lenged businesses and took a terrible job with a distressed art company just to get back in the arena (plus I desperately needed a paycheck). Eventually, my father gave me the boost of confidence I needed to launch my own consulting business focused strictly on corporate turnarounds. Five lean months later I landed my first real assignment, a Detroit machining company whose sales had dropped 90% in nine months. The bank was hostile and moving aggressively toward liquidation, and the owner was leaving for three months of intensive cancer treatments. I hit that place with a vengeance and dug in for the battle of my life. For the creditors we were just another Detroit business going down the tubes in 2009, but for me and 80 families it was personal; this was the rematch I'd been obsessing over for years. I went straight for the jugular, every jugular, and they went straight for mine. I was there to save 80 jobs, but I was also there for vengeance, and this heartless, bureaucratic banker was merely a proxy for the heartless, bureaucratic bankers I had to deal with in my own insolvent company. I was punching through targets trying to reach back and alter history. It was a street fight, but it worked. We turned profitable in month two and stayed that way. The business healed me as much as I healed it and I left Detroit with a calm confidence that I hadn't known in a very long time.

For 18 years now, I've worked exclusively in distressed businesses, five on my heels as an outgunned, stressed-out entrepreneur, and the last 13 on my toes as a corporate turnaround specialist helping entrepreneurs keep their businesses, wealth, and dignity intact. This book is written for the beleaguered entrepreneur that I once was and all the ones I hope to help over the rest of my career. This is the book I should have read before I first personally guaranteed corporate debt. It's a complete primer on fighting your way out of corporate distress, saving jobs, fortunes, and the communities they support.

Turnarounds versus Corporate Change

In my MBA program, we studied corporate change agents, the people who initiated and championed change in big corporations – you know, the crowd celebrated in pop management literature. But this is as deep as our study went: heroic characters like the team who launched Post-it Notes off 3M's massive and stable balance sheet. We never touched on insolvency or distress and we darn sure didn't discuss personal guarantees and debt collection. It's as if we studied life without ever considering illness and death.

Despite this failing in education, everyone pretty much knows that corporate turnarounds happen and are generally a good, though uncomfortable, thing. Turnaround is an imprecise term in corporate parlance. Sales managers claim a turnaround when they increase the top line. Presidents and general managers claim a turnaround when they produce significantly better profits and CEOs when they produce a significantly stronger balance sheet. Most mainstream business books and magazines have a loose definition of turnarounds ranging from banal change to trauma surgery, each associated with symptoms of decline.

Turnarounds are often like a corporate illness; sometimes a person or business just gets a bit of malaise and they need a little pick-me-up to regain focus and motivation. Sometimes the underlying issues are more serious, like flattening sales, where we just need to get the top line growing again. Turnarounds get interesting as the problems stack up; combine your malaise and softening sales with growing overhead.

Throw in margin compression and factory bottlenecks and you start needing some real turnaround expertise. The problem here is that the entrepreneur or CEO has probably never been through this before and probably doesn't really understand the balance sheet as well as they should (I didn't). So, the CEO bravely tinkers with the business but doesn't move out ahead of the problems.

But imagine that, as a CEO, you've persevered in maintaining your entrepreneurial optimism and remained convinced that the angel of good fortune will return to you as she had at other critical times in the past. But this time she's late and you just lost a key employee, customers have taken you off the bid list, and vendors are shutting you off. This is when you are sliding on ice, turning the wheel of your car, pumping the brakes but not changing the business's dangerous trajectory.

At some point, you'll trip one of the financial covenants in your loan agreement, which means it's very late in the game, because these are backward-looking formulas. The game-changer is tripping the approximately 1.2 minimum debt service coverage ratio, which is a trailing 12-month calculation, so it's old news by the time you trip it. When this happens, you'll be called to the carpet at your friendly neighborhood bank. This is an awful experience, but in reality, it is great news because you now have concerned and committed partners focused on your business. They exert all sorts of pressure and may hand you the name of a turnaround consultant. Because they are a bank, the consultant they recommend will likely be a vetted and experienced professional who they trust in situations like yours.

You will suspect this person is an agent for the lender and working counter to your interests; it's only natural to have that suspicion. I've found that most turnaround specialists are more like surgeons – trusted professionals who are fully committed to your long-term survival, regardless of your personality or how much near-term pain you'll have to endure.

The worst crisis situations require a special breed of turnaround pro, someone with a perverse love of the challenge and a deep emotional commitment to their work (a grudge from prior failure helps). Imagine you've got all the troubles we've previously discussed and then federal agents raid the facility. Customers scatter, the lender calls the loan, the union is unpaid, the IRS is foreclosing, 401k trust funds are missing, your accounting is a disaster, and vendors all hold you hostage. There are actually people who can't stop smiling when they get to fix these disasters. The higher the flames the happier they are walking in the front door.

This book discusses the techniques, tactics, and strategies deployed in the most pressing turnaround situations because a good crisis amplifies issues and brings about clarity. Collecting receivables more quickly is interesting in a huge corporation because you're saving a few days of interest on the receivable balance. Failing to collect sooner has zero downside risk. Collecting receivables in a crisis might keep the lights on while your downside risk is oblivion. When the utility shut-off crew shows up in your parking lot you only have one option, you must write them a check on the spot – and then run to find the cash to fund that check within the next couple of hours. You will either fund that check or surrender to your creditors. That clarity of mission helps everyone appreciate the value of collecting receivables. In a financial crisis, most downside repercussions are fatal, but I think that helps the organization focus, prioritize, and develop a clear understanding of what's at stake.

Whoa, I Didn't See This Coming

At 35 years of age I was rudely introduced to the world of turnarounds. It was our family business. Sales had tanked and our bank was upset. It suddenly dawned on me: "Hey wait, these guys are playing tackle and I thought we were playing touch, plus I don't know a darn thing about fixing companies." But how could that be? I had an economics degree and an MBA and spent eight years working outside the family business for companies ranging from Fortune 300 to a biotech startup. I'd read all the pop-management books and subscribed to several business magazines. And nowhere in all of that had I learned to run a business in distress. I went home and thumbed through every college textbook and business book I owned – nothing. The next day I went to the local mega bookstore, which had four bookcases full of management books and not a single title on turnarounds. We know that every company goes out of business eventually and we know that down is half of any cycle, but no one seemed to talk about it.

The lack of knowledge is so pervasive that corporate managers rarely know they have this educational deficiency until they are in deep trouble. And when they find themselves in a workout they don't know how to get out, don't know where to go for resources, and few even know the key search terms to find help online. In my first turnaround, we made it to Stage 4 (out of 5) before I learned there were even stages in a turnaround and what they were. We were a year or two into our turnaround before I stumbled on the Turnaround Management Association (TMA; www.Turnaround.org) and got myself oriented.

The TMA tests on the five stages of distress for their certification program, but they were first detailed by Donald B. Bibeault in his seminal work on the subject; *Corporate Turnaround: How Managers Turn Losers into Winners* (McGraw-Hill, 1981):

1. Management change

2. Quick evaluation

3. Emergency action

4. Stabilization

5. Return to normal growth

The book I am writing takes the reader through those stages, though not formally because the true joy and artistry of corporate turnarounds is the creative dance in that very thin space between the hammer of your creditors and the anvil of insolvency law. Cash gives you that space, and understanding the following two core principles is the key to saving a business when all the odds are stacked against you.

Two Core Principles Needed to Understand Corporate Distress

There are only two types of turnaround: (1) income statement turnarounds or (2) balance sheet turnarounds. Both necessitate positive cash flow. The former involves running out of cash from losses and about to stall mid-flight. The latter may involve a stabilized business with suffocating levels of debt. Maybe half of my clients have suffered from both ailments at the same time. Both problems present themselves in a cash crisis so the initial solution is the same – control and grow cash. Managing the cash conversion cycle (CCC) gives a company the cash it needs to survive the early days of a turnaround, whereas the priority of debt (debt stack) determines who can seize your assets and who gets paid in the debt restructuring. These two core principles underlie everything in this book which is why we're going to spend a little time here in review. Once you understand these principles the rest of the book will fly.

Cash Conversion Cycle

The cash conversion cycle (shown in Figure 1.1) is the single most reliable, simple, immediate, and valuable lever in all of business. If I had to live an entire business career with only one tool it would be this one, hands down. If you manage your cash conversion cycle well, you can literally shift millions of dollars of cash from other people's businesses into yours. But if you screw it up, you can do the opposite and quickly go bust.

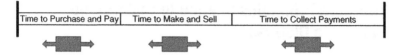

Figure 1.1 Cash conversion cycle.

The CCC is your cash-exposure window, the number of days that the working capital of your business is tied up funding the operations of that business. It's the time and money invested in turning iron ore into a new car rolling off the showroom floor. It is the time needed to sell your inventory plus the amount of time needed to collect receivables minus your vendor payment terms. Each of these factors are variable and as a CEO you can influence each to your advantage. If you can pay more slowly for expenses, it keeps cash on your balance sheet and off your suppliers. If you collect more quickly, it moves cash from your customer's balance sheet onto yours. When you need the cash more than them, you should "borrow" from them. The core of a turnaround is shifting your balance sheet to absorb the impacts of distress, then shifting back toward reinvestment and recovery, and managing the CCC is the quickest way to achieve that.

The formula for the cash conversion cycle is:

Cash Conversion Cycle

= Inventory Conversion Period (make and sell)

+ Receivables Collection Period − Payables Deferral Period

Each variable is measured in days.

Inventory Conversion Period = (Avg.Inventory/Daily COGS)

= # Days

Receivables Collection Period = Receivables/Daily Sales

= # Days

Payables Deferral Period = Payables/

Daily Cost of Goods Sold

= # Days

I'm currently involved with the restart of a steel fabrication business that went bust and stuck the vendors with more than $10 million in write-offs, so vendors are being miserly in extending us new credit. We can buy steel rolls from the distributors (service centers) with 30-day payment terms, but they don't always have what we need and we're paying a lot more than going direct to the steel mills. But the mills won't give us any credit and, in fact, are making us pay cash in advance (CIA) because they are so credit averse with an unproven company. This means paying 45 days *before* we will receive the product. So between paying 45 days before delivery to the mills or 30 days after delivery with the service centers, our choice is price versus 75 days of cash. It's a metric that changes daily (see Figure 1.2).

A 12-week delivery time is the historically fastest attainable speed in this highly engineered, heavily regulated, little niche of the steel fabrication business. Over decades, this company and our competitors have wavered between a low

Days	−45	−30	−15	0	15	30
Payables	CIA			COD		Net 30

Figure 1.2 Range of days payable.

ship time of 12 weeks and highs as much as 36 weeks. This in-between period of time, the 24 weeks between 12 and 36, is all cash-consuming waste. Every week is an extra week of payroll and supplies. Every month is an extra month of utilities, rent, insurances, and other operating expenses.

We rebuilt this company from a dead stop and quickly brought it back to breakeven, but then sales stalled and we just bumped along at breakeven for a few months, never accumulating enough cash to move to the steel mills and lower our costs or to invest in upgrades of equipment or people. Then sales tripled, which put a big strain on cash because we needed to buy more rolls of steel. We knew we were entering a virtuous profit cycle, but we needed the cash to do it. The weaknesses in our production system started to reveal themselves. Shipping times grew from 16 weeks to 20, then 24 weeks. We're clubbing it back down now from a high of 26 weeks as I write this.

Those 10 extra weeks (70 extra days) was pure cash burn. It's 70 days of not shipping but still incurring expenses daily. We'll get that cash back as we reduce our ship times (converting inventory more quickly), and with growing sales and growing margins, there's a lot of sunshine on the other side of this challenge (see Figure 1.3).

Days	10	20	30	40	50	60	70	80	90	100
Inventory										

Figure 1.3 Inventory conversion cycle – time to make and sell.

Days	10	20	30	40	50	60
Receivables						

Figure 1.4 Receivables collection period.

Our products are components of much larger commercial projects performed by deep-pocketed government contractors and deep-pocketed integrators, so although they are currently pounding on us for the delayed shipments, they are also paying us on expedited terms to help get us through this cash crunch. Our ability to collect faster is the only offset to these Payable and Inventory issues (see Figure 1.4).

Obviously, our steel fabrication business is an expensive model to operate and fund, but it is typical of most industrial businesses. A retailer gets paid at the cash register, so they don't have the collection period. It is the same with most consumer-facing businesses. For them managing the CCC is all about inventory management. Bananas and apparel both need to be sold before they go bad or out of style, hotels and restaurants need to manage their inventory of empty rooms and seats. A grocer may be turning milk inventory daily, for cash at the cash register and then paying the dairy on five-days terms, meaning that the grocer has a four-day positive cash cycled on its milk business. Software businesses will have a large sunk development cost but no real conversion cycle and no collection cycle. Automatic prepay subscription businesses with no physical assets and generous vendor payment terms are the ideal cash machines.

Debt Stack

My favorite legal axiom in insolvency is the Absolute Priority of Debt Rule. It's absolute and sets the priority of debt so no one needs to argue about who's getting paid first or who can foreclose on assets. It's all in the loan documents and on file in public UCC-1 filings (liens). Our family business sold to Kmart, and we got burned for $300,000 in their bankruptcy. I was young, so I acted emotionally; let's go sue, take up arms, sully their good name, and so on. We wasted money having our lawyer check things out. I was new to the game of insolvency, but the law is not. Banking goes back to 5,000 BC, and I suspect collateral is discussed in *Genesis*. The rules of who gets paid, how, and when have been established through millennia, and that's why it's called the Absolute Priority of Debt Rule. Talk to your lawyer, then swallow your outrage and take your position in line.

For clarity, any commercial debt stack must first pay all earned wages. This is an absolute in the United States and most other countries, and earned wages are assumed to have been fully paid in the following discussions. Beyond wages, there is a stack of debt with the senior secured lender in first position. Two more easy terms to figure out; this party is both senior and secured, so they have first collateral lien positions on the company's assets. This is typically commercial loan(s) from your local savings bank. The junior secured position is similar, though they have accepted a position subordinate to the senior but above every one else. The secured position is so revered that even the most aggressive federal collection agencies will respect the lien position and not use their unlimited powers to usurp the senior secured lender's position. This means that the IRS and the Environmental Protection Agency (EPA) will generally sit behind the senior secured creditor.

A simple private company will have leveraged (borrowed against) their Accounts Receivable and Inventory with what's called a Revolver or Revolving Loan (the balance fluctuates or "revolves" with collateral values). Additionally, they're also probably borrowing against fixed assets (equipment, real estate, intellectual property, etc.) and paying that out over a set term of years. This is called a Term Note because it's for a term or number of years and then terminates. The structure mirrors the useful life of the assets that collateralize the loan: long-term borrowing on long-term assets like machinery and short-term (revolving) borrowing for short-term assets like inventory and receivables. So one loan is backed by a senior secured position on short-term assets (Accounts Receivable and Inventory) and the other loan is backed by a senior secured position on long-term assets (machinery). A mortgage may hold a senior secured position on the real estate as well. So potentially, three senior secured lenders, each with first positions on distinct assets of the business. These three lenders will file paperwork at the county court house for each individual loan, establishing UCC-1 liens against each group of assets. Then it is public record, established by date of filing, for who has what liens and positions on what assets of what companies.

Our fictitious company anticipates growth and gets a second level of debt. This may be from a merchant's cash advance

(MCA) company they heard advertised on the radio. The MCA lender files second-position liens on the assets of the company that establishes them as the second or junior or subordinated secured lender and assures that if there was a sale or liquidation, 100% of the money would flow to the account balance of first-position lenders (Lender 1) and once their account was paid in full, 100% of what remained would flow to the account balance of second-position lenders. Sometimes much money flows to and beyond Lender 2, and sometimes none at all with a deficiency to Lender 1, even as secure as they once were.

Occasionally a $100-million-sized business will have third-level secured creditors and often they are state economic development type lenders, a second merchants cash-advance lender, mezzanine debt, or even a savvy father-in-law who lent you money and filed a lien to protect himself. It could also be a vendor or landlord who somehow negotiated their way up the debt stack and secured a claim on business assets, something you would have agreed to. In all these cases, the company (the borrower) explicitly grants rights to the lender or merchant to place liens on the company's assets as part of the loan documents or commercial contracts. If the borrower defaults on a loan, the lender can foreclose on the collateral that backs that loan. Even a third-level lender can foreclose on the assets, causing great distress to the borrower.

Credit cards are personally guaranteed by personal assets (this is often unknown and usually by the majority shareholder, whoever signed the credit card application and supplied a social security number), which means that, if a company defaults, the shareholder is getting sued personally for collection. All the sudden assets like your house, car, paycheck, and savings can be in play.

The tier below secured lenders is unsecured lenders. These are usually vendors who extend you trade credit as part of their commercial relationship. If terms of a sale are not specified (often on the purchase order or invoice) then the Uniform Commercial Code (UCC) specifies standard terms of trade within industry. For the seller, extending credit terms is part of their business plan and factored into their model (their days in their own cash conversion cycle). They manage the risk of this small window of credit, usually only 30 to 45 days, to fund what is usually a profitable multiyear supply business. While a bank can lend a lot of money very quickly and have tremendous exposure, vendor credit is usually managed and moderated and is rarely even half of the annual contribution margin generated by the sales to that customer. In a low-interest-rate environment, extending credit might be a very inexpensive way to compete with a competitor's low price or lock in volume from a customer. There is risk, of course, which is why sellers manage these accounts closely. Unsecured creditors are usually all equal in status and they are called the *general unsecured* class of creditors. This is the bottom of the debt stack, and if money flows past the secured creditors to the general unsecureds, it is distributed pro rata amongst them.

To recap, if Creditor 1 doesn't get paid in full, Creditor 2 gets nothing. If Creditor 2 isn't paid in full, Creditor 3 gets nothing. If all the secured creditors are not paid in full, then no money flows to the unsecured creditors. You can see the risk.

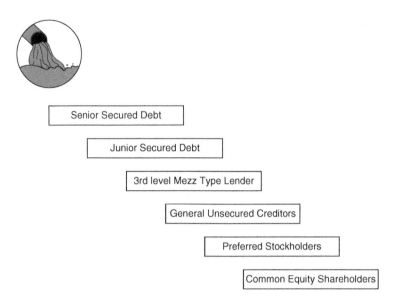

Senior Secured Debt

Junior Secured Debt

3rd level Mezz Type Lender

General Unsecured Creditors

Preferred Stockholders

Common Equity Shareholders

Figure 1.5 Example private company debt stack.
Credit: Tatum Sands

Figure 1.5 illustrates the debt stack of a midsized private company. A large public company or a private venture-funded business will both likely have a more complicated debt stack, perhaps with bonds or multiple levels of debt, and preferred and common stock.

Now that you're refreshed on some basic concepts, let's examine how you may have slipped into trouble in the first place.

23 Business Killers

Before we get started on the turnaround, let's step back and consider how we may have gotten into trouble in the first place. Some businesses are terribly resilient; they can mismanage time and again, while the customers keep coming back for more; whereas other businesses might be in a shrinking industry in which any trip-up might be fatal. Business distress is a natural state of being just as our body aging is the natural course of events for humans. Sure, we can fight decline, but we all know how the movie ends – entropy. The knowledge I share in this book won't change physics but it will give a business a clean bill of health, several more years of vitality, plus the strength and vision to fight future battles. But let's face it, the following challenges never go away. In no particular order, here is a list of landmines that scatter the field of business and human behavior:

1. **Failure to adapt.** Despite popular misconception, Darwin never said it was the strong that survive, but the adaptable. The economy is always in flux; how we read and react to that change determines our longevity.

2. **Bad luck.** A motivational speaker might tell you there is no such thing as luck, *luck comes from preparation*, or something shallow like that. But mention a factory fire, loss of health, natural disaster and everyone acknowledges that bad luck exists, and sometimes it finds you.

3. **Undercapitalized.** Occasionally I judge business-plan competitions, and not once have I seen a hopeful entrepreneur ask for enough money. A strong balance sheet will get you through the worst storms in business. My opinion is that in turnarounds luck

tends toward the downside, and you need to quickly accumulate the capital to survive those jolts.

4. **Overlevered.** Similar to undercapitalized but more dangerous. Dancing too close to the edge leaves no margin for error.

5. **Not diversified.** Investors discount the value of a business based on the risk of customer, vendor, or product concentration, or an overreliance on key employees or markets. These are real risks, and as the CEO it's your job to minimize risk throughout the organization.

6. **Lacking controls.** Running a business is more complex than flying an airplane. I've student-flown a couple of airplanes, and I prefer a working instrument panel when I do; things like altitude and airspeed are as important as cash flow and backlog when running a business. For many businesses it's the lack of controls that gets them in trouble, they simply don't see trouble developing and often misread the magnitude when they do. The ideal formula for avoiding trouble in your business is relevant measurements and timely reporting followed by swift corrective measures.

7. **Overanalyzing.** I was recently in a company that measured so much I couldn't make sense of it and neither could management. Profits swung $8 million in one year and 87 different metrics pointed to 87 different symptoms, which made simple problems even more confusing.

8. **Low gross product margin (GPM).** Sales minus the variable cost of your product or service, it's the money

you have left over for everything else, namely overhead and profits. GPM is the first number I look at when analyzing a business. Every industry and business model has a standard GPM range that the industry runs on. You should be in the high end of that range.

9. **Falling sales.** Hear the alarm bells? If your airplane is mysteriously losing altitude don't expect that it will mysteriously gain altitude next year. Talk directly to your customers to find out why sales are down.

10. **Rising costs.** This could be the pricing on commodity inputs, foreign currency exchange rates, or just the uncontrolled escalation of American healthcare costs. Rising costs need to be fought aggressively and quickly passed on to your customers.

11. **Owner health.** It's everything. I know an entrepreneur who was bedridden and out of sorts due to some strange neurological issue that was set off by turnaround stress. Only after 18 months did doctors stumble upon the correct diagnosis and treatment. Healthy people have a hundred wishes, unhealthy people only have one.

12. **Owner distraction.** Is the owner off enjoying his first boat, second home, third wife, and no longer grinding it out in the shop? The bank notices that you're off enjoying their money and so do your employees.

13. **Overexpansion.** Nations and businesses both fail by living beyond their means. If nothing else, in business always remember that neither good times nor bad last forever.

14. **Overcomplicating.** Business is simple: buy low, sell high, keep most of the spread. Don't lose sight of that, it's a simple mechanism that needs to produce cash. Too often, we see meticulously crafted financial statements with big year-end adjustments. They are "wrong to the penny." If you can't explain it to your board in one typed page, you probably shouldn't be doing it. I heard a story of a billionaire who was building a new pulp and paper mill and had brought in a team of experts to manage the project. As experts do, they complicated the heck out of an already complex project. Frustrated, the billionaire slammed his hand on the table and asked, "What the heck does any of this have to do with making me piles of money?"

15. **Regulators.** Cultivating a friendly relationship goes a long way. Much more on this in Chapter 6.

16. **Failure to control a crisis.** Stuff happens, how you react will magnify or reduce the danger.

17. **2009 credit market.** Hopefully we'll never see that again but let it be a reminder.

18. **Management transition.** Management changes are always risky. Recruiters tell me that the odds of hiring the right new general manager or president through an expensive and exhaustive retained search is only 40%.

19. **Reading too much pop-management.** Yes, that young bring-your-dog-to-work, flip-flop-wearing entrepreneur made the cover of some magazine. But the tight-fisted 60-year-old entrepreneur in your town's industrial park has proven the ability to create

generational wealth through decades of turmoil. He's not making magazine covers but he's got no debt.

20. **Falling in love with your product.** Like your own kids, they are perfect in your eyes, but maybe not in the consumer's eyes. Nothing kills the ability of a business to pivot more than an entrepreneur's adoration of his product.

21. **Entrepreneurial stubbornness.** Your enviable ability to grind through obstacles has taken you this far, but in a turnaround situation, stubbornness can become a liability. Your customers, employees, and vendors may admire and support your stubbornness, but your bank expects nimble-footed compliance and better results. Doubling down on the same old thing now will kill your credibility.

22. **Pain tolerance.** Similar to stubbornness, but worse. At some point, everyone knows you're failing but you. Everything is going south, the bank is twisting your arm but you're tough, you're gritting your teeth and enduring the pain, proudly pushing ahead on your chosen (reckless) path. The bank, your employees, your customers and vendors, they all want you to stop, accept reality, and change direction, but you just barrel on ahead. Things get worse and you just grit your teeth tighter. Eventually this gets resolved in one of three ways: the entrepreneur relents, the bank has you locked out of your own business (called receivership), or you sneak past both obstacles and destroy the business on your own.

23. **Leadership.** You are the only one who signed the personal guarantee and you are the only one who might be driven into personal bankruptcy. This is not the time for group decisions. Your neck is in the noose and your management team is most worried about keeping their jobs, it's a conflict of interest that the entrepreneur must solve.

Warning Signs

Yes, we should have seen trouble coming but we didn't. Looking back the warning signs were all there but often they were noticed too late (poor reporting) or the entrepreneur just failed to recognize their magnitude. A list of common warning signs are:

- Loss of customers, decline in bid requests, shrinking average ticket price, or lack of new product development.

- Declining gross profit margin, expanding overhead, increasing commodity prices, shifts in the market place, or foreign exchange rates, and so forth.

- Loss of key employees, increased turnover, losing key sales people, or changes in marketing.

- Distraction of owner or key executive, softening of the scrappy entrepreneurial culture or complacency.

The Job Ahead

Okay, so now you're in a turnaround situation. You've got jobs to save, debts to service, your own neck in the noose, and you'll have to break some eggs to make this omelet. Yesterday you were a kind and generous business owner. Euphemisms like, "I don't need the best deal, only a good deal" really appealed to you and you tried to lead your company like it was part of a wider economy where your vendors need to make a good margin, your employees deserve a good living, and your customers need a good price. Well, they all accomplished that and now you're the clown in workout. You know that old adage that if you don't know who the sucker is at a poker table, it's probably you? They're not in workout, you are. They're not going home to study bankruptcy schedules, to tell the wife to sell her jewelry, and wonder what your house might fetch at auction – you are.

The turnaround process is always the same, but what you have to work with never is. If I have cash and lots of options then success is almost a guarantee. If the owner/manager has burned up all his credit and goodwill waiting for the order fairy to show up, then we have significantly less to work with. In the first hour of any turnaround I try to ascertain the following factors that will influence my prospects for success:

- **Does your business even have a reason to exist?** Seriously, are you selling typewriters in 1998? Are you a small, nothing special retailer in 2017? If you are, a dignified exit may be your best alternative.

- **Time and creditor anger.** Which creditors are upset and how long have they been upset? If you're just lapsing over 30 days in payables, then we have plenty of time. If both your bank and the IRS have run out of patience, we need to move quickly.

- **Personal guarantees and regulators.** Both can bury the entrepreneur and cause him to lose hope. If his house is being foreclosed on by multiple creditors, I will struggle to keep him focused at work. The ability to keep the entrepreneur engaged is often critical to the turnaround process.

- **Mental health of the CEO.** Is the CEO clear-eyed, paying attention, and willing to do tough things, quickly? If I have a soldier ready to sacrifice for victory, then we can achieve great things together. But often CEOs, especially entrepreneurial founders, are self-destructive, usually it's passive-aggressive behavior (denial, pride, confusion, fear) but occasionally you have either a sociopath (I've had a few) or some spiraling-out-of-control behavior (I had one who ended up in the psych ward after I walked off the job). Unsurprisingly, good old-fashioned vice can also bring people down. True story: my friend owned a company located in another state, his CEO had become increasingly erratic with tales of "lady friends" visiting his corner office midday for long locked-door meetings. Eventually the CEO and his "lady friends" moved into the trailer behind the factory and didn't emerge for four days – until the owner showed up and fired him.

- **Cash flow and balance sheet.** Cash is your oxygen, the business will not survive without it and you'll need to convert your balance sheet into cash. If that's not enough, you'll need to convince your customers and vendors to convert their balance sheets into cash for you to use for your business. A few quick questions will help me determine how much room is available here.

- **Crisis readiness of your team.** Sometimes companies are filled with average people who really want to win. They may not be the all-star team, but they're tired of losing and are seriously committed to saving the business. I see this more in rural areas with few good options for alternate employment and a strong natural work ethic. The opposite can be true in strong union towns.

- **Prospects for a sale.** If all else fails, can we sell the business to protect jobs, vendors, community, and so on? I could still sell a small print shop in 2017 but might not be able to in 2027.

- **Your industry and the available levers.** Ask me to fix an operating factory with a defaulted mortgage and I'll fund it by squeezing cash out of inventory, receivables, three shifts of labor, and engineering, new product development, Capex, deferred maintenance, and so on. These are short-term tactics but they are all available to me. Ask me to fix an empty commercial building and there is not much I can do other than hire a realtor. The levers available to you at the start of the turnaround will guide your strategy.

How Hard? The Ethics of Turnaround Leadership

A friend once asked me about my business of saving companies and it seemed a bit slimy to him, you know; layoffs, delayed payments, restructured debts, and so on. I make a living from other people's misfortune, and I see how that could appear predatory in some way. I was caught off guard by his comments and thought about it a bit. My father-in-law is an orthopedic surgeon, which is a magnanimous career, but let's face it, no one sees him by choice. Something pretty rotten needs to happen for him to get patients. My wife is a nurse, and as lovely as she is, healthy people never employ her. I won't equate my work to theirs, but we all help people in need for a fee and then we leave.

Years ago, I was deep in an awful turnaround. The company had failed through multiple consecutive owners over several years, and now it was our turn. Nothing worked, things fell apart faster than I could even stop them, let alone make actual progress. My partner suggested the next three extreme tactics necessary to save the business, all of which made me blanch to even consider. They were aggressive, guaranteed to horrify every stakeholder, and would risk whatever faint pulse remained in the business. Our odds of success were miniscule.

I protested. I lacked the courage to try harder. He leaned across the table, stared deep into my eyes, and said in rising tones, *"The employees cannot be sent to the unemployment line. These people have shown up for work every day for years, when they were sick, when they didn't want to. They did it to make sure product got out the door. They have given everything to this company and they deserve to have someone fight for their jobs. They've been screwed over for years because no one cared enough to fix their company. Now they want us to fight for them and that's what we must do. The vendors want us to fight for their money, the customers want us to fight for their products. They all deserve someone who will fight to the death to save this business, someone who won't get queasy when tough measures need to be taken. That's what we're here to do and that's what we're going to do."*

And we did. It was a complete bloodbath, but two months later the company turned a small profit and the turnaround had taken hold.

Now You're in a Turnaround, What Next?

First breathe deeply and summon your energy, it's going to be a long ride. My first turnaround started with an unpleasant visit from our bank. Afterward my father, brother-in-law, and I sat around, a bit dumbfounded and caught off guard. My father said, "There's nothing we can do this afternoon, go home, take your wives out for a nice dinner, explain to them that the next six months are going to be very difficult and that you'll need their love and support to get through it." Turnarounds take a heavy toll on marriages, families, and your health. They create inordinate amounts of stress and I advise CEOs to watch for it. Sometimes it's obvious, like the 70 pounds I saw a printing CEO put on in less than a year or often just the temptations of vice to relieve the stress.

Once you've got your head right, realize that this is your big-boy/big-girl day to step up. You allowed this mess to happen and you're the one who's going to clean it. At this very moment you are sitting on nearly tectonic amounts of personal power. You literally have the ability to reshape your entire life and many others by the choices you make in the coming days and weeks. Many entrepreneurs go from years of treading water to stunning wealth through the deep dark valley of a turnaround. They do this with courage and a mad obsession to make things right. The momentum you will create can shape generations of wealth. The heroic, come from behind, turnaround script is as old as humanity and is an incredibly powerful wave to ride. But it takes a big, conscious commitment. Accepting what's ahead in a turnaround is the most grown-up, adult decision a business leader can make.

Your courage will protect and immunize you from the wearying psychological grind of a turnaround. Your emotions will swirl and spike, but so will those of your employees and lenders and vendors and customers. You need to remain the coolest head of all of them. This is your task; you need to own it and wear it fully.

Don't Be Cleopatra

It's a silly joke but one we all tell, you know she was the Queen of The Nile – Queen of Denial. Okay, it's hardly humorous but it does make the point: the sooner you face your problems, the quicker you can heal. Denial is completely natural, so expect to go through the five natural stages of grief in getting past it. The key is you just need to do it quickly. On my first turnaround, my denial was intense, and I held on hard for 24 hours before relenting. But when I broke down and accepted the situation, I quickly spun my thoughts and energies toward a solution. Often debtors can waste precious months clinging tight to their delusion while hope and options fade.

Debtor Psychology

Another old joke in our business is that turnarounds are 50% operational, 50% financial, and 50% debtor psychology. In the United States and many Western countries, the debtor stays in control through the insolvency process so you have the person who got us in trouble responsible for getting us out of trouble. Getting them out of denial and back into reality is paramount to saving the business.

The U.S. system in particular is heavily weighted toward liberty, which allows business owners to get fatally out of control before anyone can reel them in. Banks are working on trailing 12-month averages, CPAs don't seem to be proactive in these situations, and business managers are really on their own to see trouble coming and react to it.

When first hit with poor results, some managers react like they touched a hot stove and quickly seek help to relieve the pain. These are the folks who have successful turnarounds, they are completely tuned in and run back to safety. Others go sailing off the cliff like Thelma and Louise. Some charge toward the cliff, teeth gritted, hands clenched, totally vapor-locked in determination mode. No amount of information is going to overcome their stubbornness. Other debtors spin like a car sliding on ice toward the cliff peacefully oblivious to the situation. The difference in reaction magnifies quickly with time. One week later, the poor reaction is another week in trouble, whereas the wise reaction has enjoyed a week of recovery. In a month, the businesses can be worlds apart, one saveable and the other not.

Sociopaths often borrow money to start a business, leveraging many of their natural talents to do so. And when they end up in workout, all their ugliest traits come to the surface. A very thin sliver of entrepreneurs enjoyed success before going crazy and ending up institutionalized. They usually fall through my professional neighborhood on that journey.

Managers in Denial

I recently had a CEO who desperately wanted to "get it" and not be in denial. He felt so bad about having been an overbearing manager that, in a fit of democracy, he abdicated decision making to his management team. It was a nice instinct, but half the management team was incapable of thinking strategically and 100% were mostly concerned about protecting their own paychecks. This was like abdicating crop management to the locusts. So, they all voted to take my turnaround plan and execute it themselves, saving the company money and (more important) saving them from the sharp poke of me holding them accountable. In the first week, shipments were off 35%, but they just shrugged their shoulders. By the fifth week the company was out of money and I was called in to perform CPR. In the ninth week my emergency sale fell through, the business was immediately shut down, and all the jobs were lost.

You're No McKinsey Consultant

Several years ago a regional bank asked us to go visit one of their customers; it was the new owner of a $20 million business who had lost over $1.5 million in his first year. A quick Google search told me that the new entrepreneur had previously run two different $1 billion revenue companies with great success. He had a blue chip corporate career and had semiretired into entrepreneurship. We arrived at his business where he immediately started the lecture about how he knew what he was doing, the bank was all wrong, and he was a corporate thoroughbred if there ever was one. "I've run two different billion-dollar businesses, I produced hundreds of millions of dollars in shareholder value, I've received awards, I'm a leader in this industry," and he continued on about how his qualifications should eclipse his recent losses (if not the sun). "I've worked with plenty of consultants before, I've worked with McKinsey consultants in multiple projects and you're no McKinsey consultants, now are you?" he asked point blank, almost like poking his finger in my ribs. "No," I replied slowly, "we're definitely not McKinsey consultants. We're just the guys the bank sends in before they liquidate a business." A beautiful silence filled the air before he shifted the conversation to a more productive tone.

But he's right; turnaround folks are not your typical management consultants. In fact, I could never stomach the slow pace, theoretical nature of the work, the blah-blah-blah of it all would make me ill. Turnaround professionals are rarely consultants because they never aspired to be consultants, they are roll up your sleeves and get dirty-type fixers who prefer to move on to the next hot mess.

Your CPA

So many small bankrupt businesses have well-prepared tax returns and a very proud certified public accountant (CPA) standing behind them. Every year the telltale financials of these failing businesses pass through the hands of CPAs who dutifully prepares the tax return and does not mention the obvious distress. Or, business owners are cheap and they're not paying enough to get professional advice. Either way, the CPA firm you are working with must be scrutinized for the turnaround campaign. I've seen manufacturing companies that aren't measuring gross profit margin (the single most important number in manufacturing) because, "that's the way our accountant set it up." So, neither the CEO nor the CPA understands the business, but one of them will have signed a personal guarantee for this adventure.

Although you can trust your cardiologist with your heart or your legal issues with your lawyer, you absolutely cannot trust the numbers of your business to anyone. Ever. It's your airplane, you are the pilot, this is your control panel, and you must fly the plane with those controls. It's the only hope you have to overcome the long-odds of entrepreneurship.

Good CPAs will coach and guide the entrepreneur through cost containment and reduction strategies with some obvious advice about growing sales. This low-level intervention will keep many businesses out of the ditch and give the CEO time to develop into the position. Great CPAs will do your tax and audit/review work just fine and will provide solid, basic advice similar to what you would expect from a CFO.

The Turnaround Process

Like most things in life and business, there is a process here with turnarounds. It starts with stabilization, then generates cash to fund changes in the business. The following steps summarize the outline and chapters of this book. True success in a turnaround follows an arc from crisis to stabilization, restructuring and then new growth and security. We'll explore these much more in the coming chapters.

- **Stabilizing.** After the initial shock, we need to quickly assess the business for the biggest and most fatal wounds and apply pressure. If your biggest customer just pulled their business, you must be in their office the next day, going for broke to get them back. If you've got a regulator issue, you've got to contain it and manage the information to customers. When your lender is upset, they generally want four things: (1) respect, (2) attention, (3) collateral control, and (4) information. Like the vacationing neighbor who owes you money, the lender wants to see you worried more about its money than your lifestyle. Our goal is getting 30 days of leniency, so we can address all the issues and start a plan of remedy. This is called forbearance, during which creditors agree to forbear (defer) their right to put you out of business. There is formal forbearance during which, say, your lender will agree not to foreclose on your assets based on certain promises and fees. But in a crisis, we don't have time for a formal forbearance, we just need time to get things sorted out while trying try to save the business. Emergency lender negotiations are continuous and often sound something like this:

> Mrs. Lender, as much as we respect your right to do X, Y, and Z, we believe that would be destructive and fraught with litigation concerns. Instead we ask that you retain all power and all options but give us a mere 30 days to present you with a complete turnaround plan to address these issues and increase the odds that you get paid back …

If you still have credibility left, that's about all you've got when making that pitch. I've turned 24-hour reprieves into full months but on day one I'll take whatever we can get.

- **Overreacting**. It doesn't happen, so don't worry about it. I have yet to see an entrepreneur overcut costs or overraise prices. It's such an uncomfortable task that no one is overdoing it, but they all fear they are.

- **Creating cash**. Running a business on cash is the most familiar concept to a street merchant or hustler and the most foreign concept to a MBA or CFO. It's like running your lemonade stand out of your pocket, cash goes in and cash goes out and when you have no cash then you are broke. Creating cash is simply pulling cash off your balance sheet and the balance sheets of your customers and vendors. This cash funds the turnaround and protects value for all your stakeholders.

- **Diagnosis**. Now we're looking at the income statement (profit and loss statement or P&L) to figure out where the structural problems are in the business. The first question we need to answer is where the biggest cash drains are and make them smaller – pretty simple really. The problems are easy to identify when you've been in enough businesses and industries. Declining sales are an obvious problem. My second question is what the GPM (gross profit margin) is and then benchmark that against what we know of the industry and business model. Low GPM means the company's either not charging enough or is very inefficient in what it makes or provides. If the former, they probably have a timid sales department. If the latter, they have either not reinvested in production technology or they have a weak production culture. The third question is overhead (if my GPM is solid, what's eating up the profits?). The biggest categories are going to be labor, insurances, facilities, interest. They probably all need work, but figure out which are the biggest holes.

- **Reorganizing.** Once you're able to stabilize revenue, how much of a business can that revenue level actually support? If revenues were sawed in half, how do you adapt and reorganize your business around that new paradigm? (Hint: hoping for revenues to bounce back is not an option.) If you don't know what revenue is going to be, make a conservative guess and build a plan to be profitable around that. This is not a budgeting exercise, it's about forecasting cash flows and finding ways to stay cash positive throughout. It is not always pretty.

- **The turnaround plan.** This is the plan that you sell to the lenders, vendors, employees, key customers, and so on. Let me be clear, you are not presenting this plan, you are *selling* it. It has to be better than a liquidation and be simple to understand; we're cutting costs here and raising prices there. The turnaround plan should be complete and presentable as a draft within 30 days of formal turnaround work beginning. The turnaround plan details what's working and what's not in the business, what activities/products/investments will be grown, which ones will be fixed, and which ones exited. The expectation is that the business will become accrual-based profitable the month the turnaround plan is enacted. When you can bring stakeholders a plan that requires no additional cash and fixes the business in 30 days, it's hard not to get support. This plan may include a shared sacrifice program between employees, customers, vendors, and lenders but the key is identifying and detailing how the company can stay open.

- **Executing the turnaround.** With a good plan and support of your creditors, now you can start to execute. Best to move quickly and do as much as you can all at once. If your plan calls for mass layoffs, closed divisions, higher prices, and so on – do it all at once. Shock the system then focus on recovery. This is ripping all the bandages off at once. Your employees have been through enough, don't drain their psyche with the slow drip-drip of change. Once the band aids are off, focus on rebuilding confidence and morale, this is your team and you're still trying to get them to the Super Bowl. (See Chapter 5.)

- **Restructure your debts around the new business.** You need to show creditors how the business can survive, how it can regain health, and what level of debt it can repay over the next few years. Whether in or out of court, the process is similar. If the company has been crushed (i.e. lost half its revenues, needs to catch up on deferred capital investments, etc.) then it can only afford a certain amount of payments for principle and interest annually. Maybe all this requires is for the lenders to stretch out debts. Likely, they will need to take a principle haircut in addition to stretching out the repayment schedule. Accomplishing this is mostly psychological, if you're defaulting on corporate debt but still rolling up to the country club in your Maserati (like my client did) the lender will torture you. If you're like my father in his turnaround who sold his $200,000 Lexus, bought a VW and put the cash difference into the business, then the lender knows you respect its money, are committed to the process, and are working with them. (See Chapter 8.)

- **Growing or selling the business when the turnaround is complete.** Whew, breathe deep again, just like when you started this perilous journey. When I got to this point in our own turnaround, it was like the storm clouds had finally parted and the sun was poking through. Our revenues were growing, employees were smiling again, our new product-development backlog was at an all-time high, and we were prebooking orders at a record-setting pace. Our balance sheet was still heavily levered but everything else was great. So I went on a long and remote vacation to celebrate, restore and get ready for our busy fall season. Then Hurricane Katrina rolled in and reset the clock.

A Word on Professional Help

I wish we had hired a turnaround consultant (also called a chief restructuring officer (CRO) or turnaround manager) after Katrina. My brains were scrambled and an objective, experienced advisor could have improved our outcome by several million dollars. Sometimes a turnaround professional is an insurance policy, someone who might double your odds of success going through a 90-day transition with perilous risks. Turnaround consultants are hired gun advisors who rest up between assignments, so they can give their clients extraordinary levels of effort and attention when needed.

The best resource for identifying turnaround consultants is through the Turnaround Management Association, which administers the industry certification, called the Certified Turnaround Professional (CTP). Certification is earned through a series of exams, validated experience, peer and client reviews. The three exams cover

1. Commercial, insolvency, and bankruptcy law.

2. Accounting, financial analysis, cash forecasting, commercial finance, and valuation.

3. Turnaround management and the ability to rapidly reshape an organization.

Applicants also must have led a certain number of verifiable turnarounds in their career and have interacted with enough other insolvency professionals to support their accomplishments with peer and client reviews. With equal amounts of law, finance, and management experience, turnaround experience often takes decades to develop. A recent check on the TMA roster showed there were 364 CTPs in the United States. Like all other professionals, you should screen them for a track record of results, reputation, industry experience, and personal chemistry.

Chapter 2

Crisis Leadership

The best turnarounds often start with a shock, something that breaks through the clutter and distraction of the languishing business and refocuses the team's attention. Not being able to fund payroll is a common financial crisis. Losing a major customer or a key employee can jolt a workforce as well, and a good leader knows how to manage and refocus the anxiety that accompanies these sorts of disruptions. Good leaders never let a crisis go to waste, while poor leaders are overwhelmed in a crisis, often losing control (and their jobs). How a leader responds at the moment of shock magnifies the results going forward.

If there is no natural crisis but the leader is authentically ready for a change, then sometimes a shock needs to be created. When you tell people they need to change, they hear you but usually don't really take it seriously. When you fire their boss or shut down a division and then tell people things need to change, they usually pay attention.

The critical first step in any crisis is to establish control. Control of your thoughts and your reactions first. Control of cash, customers, and employees next.

Day 1: Cash and Controls

Priority 1 is to establish full control over cash and collateral. Do it immediately, in the first five minutes. There are only three things that can shut a business down immediately:

1. Lack of cash (Chapter 3)
2. The bank (Chapter 4)
3. Regulators (Chapter 6)

If you respect and control the bank's cash and collateral, it will work with you, but you've got to establish that control immediately. This is as simple as dollars-in and dollars-out. Right now, Day 1, you need to control dollars out. In most cases you can make it through that first day without spending any money.

Banks secure their debts with collateral, which is the hard assets that can be foreclosed on and turned into cash, usually receivables, inventory, rolling stock (trucks, etc.), and fixed assets (equipment, real estate, intellectual property, etc.). To control receivables, make sure all shipments are invoiced and that active collection processes are in place with accounts outstanding. Inventory is first controlled with a fresh count, and then by converting it to cash and reducing the overall level. Too often in a turnaround, the accounting department is squeezing nickels trying to make payroll, while purchasing just keeps issuing purchase orders oblivious to the cash impact. Theft is another way to lose value in inventory and so is perishability (think of bananas on a shelf, losing value every day they age). Perishable stock needs to be turning at a high rate. Rolling stock is protected by securing all titles (long story, but I know a bank that lost 40 cars because they forgot to secure the titles) and inventorying all vehicles and locations. Fixed assets need to be secured against theft and also protected against loss; equipment still needs maintenance and repairs.

Cash is priority 1. Without cash the business will die, quickly. Set up check and cash approvals so that nothing can get paid without CEO approval. If you or the bank don't trust the CEO, find another way. Outside advisors will avoid check signing authority because it carries legal and regulatory risk, Federal trust-fund investigations (Chapter 6) always start by asking who had check signing authority.

Cash control is ultimately governed by the rolling 13-week cash-flow forecast (13WCFF), which is the standard model for all turnarounds. It's the first thing banks, creditors, and government agencies will ask for. Day 1 you'll need to start preparing this, which means building it out one week at a time. Oddly, there is no standard format, no Excel sheet you can download and populate. I pretty much build each cash-flow forecast by hand, from a fresh spreadsheet. In businesses with broken accounting, I've grabbed the stack of bills off the controller's desk and spent the evening typing in every vendor, dollar amount, and date. That's the beauty of the 13-week cash-flow forecast, it removes all the mystery. If you understand the cash-flow forecast you understand the business.

After cash, collateral, and regulators, the next thing to pre-serve is going concern value. This is the unquantifiable soft value of the business over and above the hard asset values. It's your customer list, your vendor relationships, employee skill, backlog, brand, reputation, and so forth. No one calls a pile of assets to place an order, but even in the worst businesses the phone still rings. There is a value to that going concern and it needs to be protected. This is mostly through communication and handling. You have to smile and promote nondeceitful confidence even when the bank is strangling you – and oddly, they expect it of you.

After Cash: Biggest Flames First

That's it, you're going to be firefighting until you can get the business stabilized. Forget strategy, forget the income statement, forget whatever you might have had planned for the next 100 days, you're firefighting. Your prima donna salesman wants to quit (to cover his own ego because he knows it's his fault that sales are down) – deal with it and keep him on board. The bank wants to drain your payroll account – deal with it. Your biggest customer wants to process a big return – deal with it. When it rains it pours, and turnarounds are hurricanes of bad luck. Keep an eye on cash and deal with everything that comes up, quickly and honestly.

Be alert and prepared to deal with whatever comes next. When a customer or employee has an issue, you need to actively soothe them. When a vendor wants to cut you off, you have to go at them full speed to explain the value of supporting your efforts. When a collector calls to scare and intimidate you, you need to throw it back in their face.

Bending the Stick

My first turnaround was our family business. We got in trouble pretty quickly, then revenues dropped 75% over the next three years. I made plenty of rookie mistakes and remember multiple times thinking "this will kill the company" as we contemplated the next survival measure. If we layoff X number of people, service will fall, customers will leave, and the business will fail. I believed the business was too fragile to take these hits as we scaled back, but it always seemed better to try than to just quit and accept whatever painful death the bank had in store for us.

So we had the second round of layoffs, prioritized important tasks, and ... and the business survived. But revenues continued to fall and eventually we were faced with oblivion again. Telling vendors we needed extra credit terms seemed suicidal; there is no way they would support us. Again, our desperation seemed certain to kill the business, but it was better than a quick trip to oblivion, so we called our vendors, told them what was happening, and suspended payments on all past-due amounts. And, miraculously, the business survived.

Revenues continued to fall, and again we faced tough tasks. Raising prices on our customers would surely kill the business; there was no way they would stick with us. But we raised prices and the business continued (healthier). After two rounds of layoffs we were down to our core group of employees; these were the very best people we had, but more cuts were in order. A 10% across-the-board pay cut would certainly send them all packing and kill the business once and for all. We did it and the employees stuck with us and the business survived.

All of this amazed me – the business was four times more resilient than I would have ever imagined. I've described this with the metaphor of bending a stick: you hold a stick, flex it a little bit in your hands and think you have a pretty good idea of how far you can bend it before it will snap. But you bend it past that point and it doesn't break. As poor results continue, you keep bending and bending. Soon your stick has bent full circle and it still hasn't snapped. Despite how fragile we believe businesses are, the best operators know how hard they can be pushed when survival is at stake.

The Psychology of Crisis Leadership

Much has been written on the topic of the psychology of crisis leadership, some of it quite good, though usually third person and a bit academic. Since I've flailed and cried and hit bottom in my own life I understand these situations well. I've also had one or two brief moments of heroic triumph that showed me what I'm capable of when my mind is clear and focused. Aside from the service academies, you are not going to find crisis leadership taught in any meaningful way at U.S. colleges, and certainly not in high school. When there is a crisis, we will react; that is certain. And it will usually be far short of our aspirations. The entrepreneur's reaction will have an outsized impact on the success or failure of the business and its survival, so there must be clarity of thought.

Crisis leadership requires quick and decisive action because bringing control to chaos is the highest priority. Although an inclusive, open management style is usually the best way to guide a stable business, turbulence requires strong and unyielding resistance. The hotter the turbulence, the more authoritarian your opposing leadership needs to be. As a leader, you need to be out in front, leading the charge and showing people what is possible. There is no such thing as leading from behind.

We've all heard the popular theory about how people respond to crisis – namely, the fight or flight model. When shocked, people's natural reaction is to fight or to run away. Picture our Neanderthal ancestors coming across a bear or mastodon or whatever. Some would stand their ground and fight; some would run away. Psychologists and pop-management gurus will carry on with this theory but I don't think it really encapsulates how people react in crisis. I find the flat squirrel theory more accurate. You know what happens when a squirrel runs out in front of your car and then has second thoughts. Some squirrels will dart off the road, while others will scurry back and forth, then get run over and become flat squirrels. Their brains get vapor locked with an avalanche of emotion and thought and the mind is no longer controlling the body. This happens to entrepreneurs.

Stories of 9/11 illustrate this. Some people ran down the stairs while others stayed put, paralyzed in fear. I saw this recently on the news after an active-shooter event in Dallas where a witness recalls running away with his son but people were standing frozen in the middle of the street. He would grab their shoulder and yell, "Run." And they would run. But short of that they were flat squirrels in the making.

A few personal experiences have helped me understand the subject well. Through a hurricane, a grizzly bear encounter, and getting clobbered mountain climbing I've learned a lot about the mind in crisis and my own fragility. This gives me some perspective on the challenges you'll face in a corporate turnaround and helps provide some context to my points.

This flat squirrel mindlock happened to me once so very acutely that I was dangerously out of control and had absolute blackout gaps in my consciousness. I was alone beneath Mt. Doonerak in far northern Alaska, about 30 miles from the only road, 60 or so miles from the nearest village (Wiseman, population 14) and a much longer distance from medical help. I had just cooked up dinner on my little camp stove when I leaned back to notice that a grizzly bear had apparently walked up and laid down right next to me, never making a sound. I noticed him out of the corner of my eye and spun around on all fours to stare him right in the face, only an arm's length away. A million (mostly dumb and unhelpful) thoughts raced through my brain as I tried to figure out what's next. A bear is most dangerous in two instances; when you're right next to him (I was) and when you're running away from him (I was about to). Quick movement away from a bear sets off their natural predatory instincts and makes them want to catch whatever is running away. So there I was kneeling in front of him, paralyzed in fear with no safe way out of this predicament.

I was kneeling there staring into his infinitely deep black eyes then my brain would go black and I would "come to" some time later and have to recalibrate my situation again. I faded in and out of consciousness a few times in the exact same place, face to face with this bear and no obvious progress between us. Other times I would "awaken" having moved a short distance and changed the dynamics of our encounter. Eventually my actions coalesced into a direction and I found myself lurching away from the bear. My mind screamed "DON'T RUN" because he would chase me if I did. So I'd stop and look to see the bear only 10 feet away tensing up as if to lunge. I breathed and relaxed to release the tension between us, which worked, but the next thing I knew, I'd be frantically dashing away again. Deep internal scream, stop, settle his tension, repeat. In extra-conscious spasms of escape, I made it across the creek bed and up a bluff. I was maybe 50 yards away from him now and settled my mind enough to look back and try to figure out my next steps. There were none; if he wanted, I'd be nothing but a grease spot on the tundra by morning. While thinking this through, I remember looking at my arms which were carpeted in mosquitoes, maybe 100 in total, and realized that I didn't feel a thing because I was so jacked up on adrenaline. Eventually the bear wandered off and I gathered up my camp and ran back toward civilization.

The point is, I've seen entrepreneurs respond like this in a financial crisis – flailing along in a state of semi vapor lock. I've done it myself in my own turnaround, so I fully appreciate the reaction. With experience, you learn how to fight the hysteria and focus in on a few productive thoughts.

An offset to that pitiful story is that one summer day I was driving between Dallas and Shreveport on a long, flat, and boring stretch of I-20. Up ahead, I saw dust, a fast-growing linear dust cloud spreading out in the median. I knew there had to be an accident, and to this day I'm amazed at the clarity that took over my mind – quite the opposite of what I experienced with the bear. A large passenger van with two mothers and about eight kids had lost control and flipped multiple times in the median, ejecting kids out windows along maybe 100 feet of the wide, grassy median while rolling. I was the first one on the scene but many others stopped soon afterward to help. The van lay on its side with children, luggage, and a few loose car parts strewn in its wake. It may have flipped six times before coming to a rest on one of the mothers.

I cannot explain my lack of control during the bear encounter nor how well I reacted in this car accident. I ran from injured person to injured person, grabbing volunteers and handing out assignments; "this girl is conscious, get her some water. You two, stand here to block the hot sun and give her shade. You, tend to her, don't move her, and watch her breathing. If you can get her to communicate take an inventory of her injuries. Write it down to give to the EMTs when they arrive. Do an inventory yourself, feel lightly with your hands for bleeding or broken bones. If there's heavy bleeding apply pressure and call out for help." Then off to the next victim, looking for life threatening injuries. Other drivers were coming to help. "Hey you two, we need help right here." Same instructions, then off to the next.

One of the mothers was trapped under the van and unconscious. I crawled underneath with another guy; she had a pulse and was breathing. We got about ten of us to roll the van off her, but she came up with her head pouring blood. I got some guy to give up his shirt and showed him how to apply pressure to her head wound. One by one, I ran around to every victim, assessed their injuries and assigned tasks to keep the injured with water, shade, and personal attention. The accident scene was now filled with motorists as traffic backed up on I-20. I assigned two bystanders to collect luggage and personal items of the victims that had been splayed across the grass. Soon after, helicopters descended on the scene and a long line of ambulances and police cars arrived. When the EMTs arrived, 10 accident victims were well tended to, each with observers and a list of injuries. All the family's personal affects had been piled up and secured. In retrospect it was the most efficient and effective moments of my life. I got back in my car and continued east toward home, totally drained.

So, I've seen myself utterly, dangerously flail in crisis and have also responded quite well. What's the difference? I don't know. But I do know that I've got both responses in me and I suspect we all do. When charged with great stress, I'll have an idea of what to expect and how I might be able to control my reactions. But we never really know how we're going to react to that first shot of adrenaline.

Hurricane Katrina was my third big event, it wiped out our neighborhood and homes, damaged our factory and scattered our employees. My reaction was sometimes brilliant (my ability to organize our neighborhood, our damaged factory, and my flooded home) and at other times pathetic (exhaustion, confusion, selfishness, crabbiness) but I got through it with about two cents, my family, a bit of PTSD, and one hell of a lot of determination to rebuild.

A Little Bit of John Wayne

A secret trick in turnarounds is that the more you act like John Wayne, the better your results will be. When trouble hits the fan, people want leadership, and in many people's mind leadership walks and talks a bit like John Wayne. One of the most powerful acts of leadership I've seen was after Hurricane Katrina when New Orleans had fallen into crisis following days of lootings and shootings. It was ugly and dangerous, and it brought out the very worst reaction from those sent to help. Instead of helping, National Guardsmen were heavily armed and fortified, pointing guns at helpless flood victims in a dangerous standoff of fear, desperation, and uncertainty. Then General Honore arrived with the presence of George Patton. He marched right between the heavily armed soldiers and the poor folks huddled outside the Superdome. "Put your guns down! Put those damn guns down! These are American citizens, put your guns down!" Within seconds soldiers had dropped their guns, walked forward and began handing out bottled water. That was it! In those 10 seconds, the entire city of New Orleans shifted from armed confrontation into recovery.

Yes, being a three-star general helps deliver orders in a crisis, but sometimes it can be subtle messages that speak loudly. After Hurricane Irene hit Vermont, there was a segment on Vermont Public Radio about guys in one town who put on orange vests and happened to have police-type ball caps – not official hats but in that style. They did this for no official reason, just to let people know they were willing to help. All day, they noticed that people were drawn to them, asking for direction and advice. So they would dispatch people to run errands and be productive. They continued to do this over the first several days and ended up in a de facto leadership role for their entire village. Regardless of the form, people seek leadership in crisis. They want to help, they just need someone to give them confidence and direction.

I once walked into a turnaround where the patriarch had died suddenly leaving three traumatized family members in the business. This coincided with the FBI investigating two financial felonies and a third felony for knowingly and willfully shipping defective airplane parts to their largest customer. Meanwhile, the business had been run into the ground, no maintenance or investment had been put into the equipment in six years, employees were upset, coming and going as they pleased, and occasionally drinking on the job. Now the patriarch was dead and the bank wanted its money. I was in there the next day, and it felt like stepping into a hurricane. I faked confidence. I told everyone things would be just fine as long as they got back to work and quit screwing around. I was totally freaked out, convinced the place was going up in flames and would take me with it. But I hid my fear and moved forward. Somehow we got through it and afterward people told me, "I thought we were done for without any hope of survival, but you were confident and that's what got us through."

My favorite contemporary turnaround character is Winston Wolfe from the movie *Pulp Fiction*. He arrives to clean up a body for Samuel L. Jackson and John Travolta at Quentin Tarantino's house. The Wolf exudes confidence, hands out orders, and doesn't skip a beat when those three clowns bumble about. It's clear that Mr. Wolfe is a highly paid professional, and he's simply there to do his job and leave.

The point in all these examples is that in moments of crisis, confidence triumphs over fear. As Winston Churchill once said; "Fear is a reaction. Courage is a decision."

Messaging to Stakeholders

When I walk in the door of a turnaround, my initial messaging is pretty close to that of Winston Wolfe. They know their jobs and the business is screwed, so I've got to get them refocused:

> I'm here because I specialize in these situations. It is all that I do, and I have a great track record. There is a process to solving these problems. It's not easy, but it is simple, so we're going to follow the process and we'll deal with surprises as they come up. This will be tough, but I've seen much worse. The whole key to solving this is focusing on doing more of what works and less of what doesn't. You folks know what's right and what's wrong; you don't need me to tell you how to do your job, so I need you to do your job exceptionally well in the next few weeks. If we keep our customers happy and don't screw anything else up, we'll probably get through this. But this week I've got to focus on keeping the bank happy and making sure payroll stays funded. That's my job. Your job is different and I need each of you to do yours.

Every employee is different but all employees need to be refocused and rehabilitated. Some have to be handled gently, and others might need a shock; others are hidden warriors and simply need direction and support.

Day 1, a small handful of employees will get a full dose of my intense focus, and they will be moved into action. This is usually the CFO and controller. They understand that the game has changed and we need to focus on priorities. Word spreads, and the message I want getting out there is this: Holy cow, this guy is unrelenting but he knows what he's doing and it all makes sense. He's also human, he has a wife and kids, he laughs and tells bad jokes.

I don't need to shock the whole organization and it's not healthy to do so. If I can smile, laugh, and make people feel comfortable while I triple their workload and hold them accountable, word will spread. An organization in change mode needs to get back a little of that "Officer on deck!" tension just to get people refocused. While I zero in on finances, I tell other departments; "tighten up now because eventually I'll get to you and want to find you doing all the right things when I get there – and, do you need any help from me today?"

My communication to the bank is open, sober, and frequent. If they didn't refer me to the turnaround position, I need to quickly establish myself and gain their confidence. See Chapter 4, which is all about dealing with banks and a new generation of institutional lenders.

Vendors

After employees and cash, I'm usually dealing with vendors as we rebuild the supply chain. I have no cash and no way to satisfy them, so I quickly say something like this:

> You don't know me but I'm the only guy who can get you paid, and the only tool I have at the moment is my credibility. If I screw that up, I'm toast, and you'll shut us off and the business will die and you'll collect nothing. But as long as I am totally honest with you, and I get your support, we can develop a plan to get you paid. But for now I've got no cash and you're underwater. As much as you may not like it, the only way out of this is that we need to work together.

Expect that you'll need to work your way up to a credit manager or the CFO or the owner, depending on the size of the business. You need someone who can understand the concepts and make decisions. Sometimes I'll need to talk with their attorney to get my point across – that they are out the money and the only chance they have of repayment is through future cash flows, which is why they need to support our efforts. Then go for the one thing you need from them today – a shipment. Explain to them the debt stack and how they effectively own the business now: "You're above equity now so you need to act like it."

In a closely held business I'm usually dealing with the majority shareholder who is the founder and patriarch. Other businesses may have active and passive partners with a variety of perspectives and risks in the business. Getting their support is usually pretty easy once they understand the rules of insolvency and how their equity is at the very bottom of the debt stack. Owners (equity) are the very last to get paid, so they have every possible incentive to make sure we turn the company around, pay down debt, and avoid personal financial ruin.

The message to customers is simply confidence and service. No panic, no alarm; insulate them from the issues, and tackle them if they try to leave.

Empathy

Perhaps it wasn't my strong suit in my twenties, but empathy may be the single most critical emotion someone can have during corporate distress. As I've matured, I realize how we all have fears, we want our spouses to respect us, and we want our kids to feel safe and comforted. I've been jobless and felt the depressing emptiness that builds each and every day out of work, burning through savings and faking courage and optimism in front of my wife and kids.

In the 1990s a guy named Chainsaw Al Dunlap rose to corporate fame as the meanest turnaround guy in corporate America. Referred to as "Rambo in pinstripes," Dunlap took pride in mass layoffs and cost cutting, and he had a good string of successes early on. To him that success justified treating people as disposable digits on an income statement. Although layoffs are a necessary part of fixing business, Dunlap enjoyed the national notoriety of being a hatchet man and allowed himself to become a caricature of heartless corporate America. He lost his humanity in the process, and it didn't make him any better at his job.

Although layoffs may be necessary, I absolutely believe that you can be the strong John Wayne–type leader and still give people hugs, know their pain, and cry with them at times. I've teared up when having to let someone go. Someone who you know is unlikely to ever find work again based on their age, location, and lack of modern skills. You can see the fear and horror in their eyes, and you need to somehow let them go, give them a hug, and boost them up so they can at least make it out to the parking lot with their head held high and their dignity intact. It's tough but necessary to save the remaining jobs.

Despair

Turnarounds are awful and you'll often have to fight feelings of despair. There will be dark moments when you can feel the walls closing in on you. Suicides happen, marriages are ruined, booze and drugs sing a tempting sirens' song of escape. It is likely that you will experience your lowest emotional points during this turnaround crisis, and your team will feel it along with you, but somehow you are the one who must pull everyone forward. This is the crucible of leadership, not being liked, not being managerial, but giving people hope and a path forward when all seems lost.

Let me share a quick story that helped me understand and fight through two grueling turnarounds of my own later in life. In our twenties, my wife Alex and I were avid mountain climbers and chose to climb a big remote Alaskan peak for our first wedding anniversary. We would spend nine days in early June under clear 24-hour skies climbing Mt. Marcus Baker, then nabbing multiple first ski descents on many of the surrounding unnamed peaks. The fantasy in our mind was amazing, and after a long Alaskan winter, our only imagined risk would be sunburn. Everything was planned down to the T and we naively expected good weather.

Our pilot flew us in about 50 miles to the upper ramparts of the Knik glacier and set down in about five feet of newly fallen snow. The enveloping silence as your bush pilot leaves you behind in big remote wilderness is always unsettling but we were young and well prepared for the adventures ahead. Alex and I set up camp, made dinner and went to sleep. During the night, a storm buried our tent, literally snow piled three feet above the roof of our tent when we woke up gasping for oxygen. We escaped upward then dug out our tent about halfway before it collapsed, jagged tent poles ripping through the thin nylon. Then we were screwed; no tent, middle of a glacier, 50 miles from the nearest road, in a hurricane force storm and totally on our own.

A snow cave was our only survival option so we dug downward, eight feet until we hit snow firm enough to form a roof, another four feet for the cave and cramped quarters underneath. After several hours of digging we had our cave and stopped to brew tea and take a break. Thirty minutes later, there was a foot of new snow piled up at our entrance, threatening to bury us well below the glacier surface. So we went back out to shovel and continued throughout the day. Twenty hours later we still hadn't had any rest longer than it took to melt snow and brew hot drinks. This meant about 30 minutes of cold, wet, shivering rest for every two hours of shoveling. At the 24-hour mark, the storm picked up intensity and we could barely keep up with the new snow. Around hour 30 we were exhausted and losing the battle, surface winds were gusting over 80 mph, visibility remained zero, snow was accumulating, and our cave entrance was filling in faster than we could clean it.

Although young and strong, we were losing steam. Through the shrieking wind Alex asked, "What happens when we can't keep up?" I mumbled something optimistic and hollow, but we both knew the answer, we would be buried and die. For hours it hung in our minds, unspoken but understood. For hours we shoveled away snow and fear with our flagging energy. The idea of being buried forever on this glacier pushed heavy against us like the incessant wind.

Even today, I sometimes feel like the turnaround will beat me, that I will fail, that all will be lost, jobs obliterated, and that I will be shamed in public, never to work again in my craft. Sometimes this feeling can last for days, following me from my hotel room to the factory and back for 16-hour days on end. But never has it weighed so heavily as those long hours on Knik glacier.

Because we eventually engineered a new cave and entrance, because after 39 hours of straight effort we were finally able to nap, because eight days later the storm finally abated, because of all that, I know that every storm will end and sunny days will return. This is the faith that allows me to infect others with my smile during the turnaround. Somehow, I can infect others with optimism that although we can't fund payroll on Wednesday we'll somehow figure out how to fund handwritten checks by Friday (or Monday). As a leader, you must be the one who shines hope through the dark stormy night. You must tamp down your own feelings of despair, because if you don't, no one else will, and all could be lost.

For now, you have to get busy fixing the business. You'll have to survey fatal threats and work off lots of detailed checklists. You will be perpetually reviewing people, products, and processes. I work outward in concentric circles, taking care of critical issues in each department before moving to second-tier issues, slowly working myself outward in priority through the departments, making sure everything stays on track. All facts need to be verified and all opinions vetted, the turnaround manager must deal with facts. I peer-review managers, continually asking, "So on a 1 to 10, how would you rate Joe?" Within a few days, I'll have many opinions on each manager, and the strengths and weaknesses of each will be obvious.

Turnarounds are an opportunity for heroes. I give plenty of speeches about how some clever employee is going to take advantage of this situation and rapidly advance their career by helping, while others sit back with an "I'll just see what happens" attitude. A few employees will see the opportunity and take matters into their own hands. I tell everyone they are free to make changes. We are determined to work smarter and if you want to make changes, come see me and I'll start approving your changes. Want to really shake things up, I'll give you all the rope you need.

Motivation

My very firm belief is that everyone wants to be on a winning team. Everyone knows what it takes and they dream of putting in that "Rocky" effort to be a winner. People in a turnaround have had big past successes in life and work, but it's probably been a while, and they've forgotten how wonderful it feels to win. Part of turnaround leadership is convincing them that now is the time for that Rocky Balboa effort.

There are a million ways to motivate people, but sometimes it's just going straight for their heart and laying it all out there for them. The stakes in a turnaround are high, and you can't screw around trying to be persuasive. When I interviewed to take on my first consulting project by the entrepreneur who was about to leave for three months of intensive cancer treatments, he played it cool throughout, as though he didn't need my help. We walked out to the parking lot as I prepared to leave, and there was the vice president of sales, Bill, and the vice president of operations being held apart from a fist fight. They each wanted blood about as bad as I've ever seen it.

We got them broken up and I followed Bill as he stormed toward his car in the back of the lot. He seemed content to fill the air with curse words and to quit right then and there in a dramatic fashion. Bill was 60 years old, ready to retire, and didn't give a hoot any more. I could also tell that Bill was a former athlete, a competitive guy, extremely proud, and a little bit hurt that he was to blame for the decline in sales. As Bill was marching to his car, I knew I had about one minute so I went for broke:

> Look, you can quit but you're going to live another 20 years, and for 20 years you're going to know you walked out of here a loser. It will haunt you, it will destroy your life and your happiness, and the regret will hollow you out inside. It will wreck your health and your relationships, and it will follow you to the grave. You will never escape it. But if you stay here and work with me, I'll help you walk out of here like the champion you are in six months. That's 20 years of feeling like a champ, holding your head high, and being a better husband and grandfather for it. Bill, you're a winner, and you need to leave as a winner. I need six months, that's it.

We beat the hell out of that business and two months later we were profitable. By month 6 our backlog was replenished, the bank was acting like our buddy again, and Bill was a hero. He stuck around another two years and retired as a champion.

Another time, I took over a remote mill that had failed. As so often happens, the union and former owners had gone through the plant like locusts, draining every last scrap of value out of a business that should have been profitable. The owners announced that the mill would be closed and dismantled, customers left, inventories were run down, local real estate prices tanked, the whole town braced for financial depression. Three weeks before the closing, a gutsy distressed investor stepped in with a plan to save the mill (and town, and region, etc.). I was put in as the turnaround agent, and my message to the 650 employees and contractors was simple:

> You just got a second chance at life. You ate fried chicken and smoked cigarettes every damn day for 20 years and you had a heart attack. Now you have to decide if you're going back to fried chicken and cigarettes or if you're actually going to get serious with your life and your career. The whole town is watching, and what I can guarantee you is that time will pass. Ten years will come, that's certain. What's uncertain is what you're going to do with it. In 10 years, are you going to walk around town with your head held high because you took control of your future? Is this mill going to be the best place to work not because it pays more than the Quicky Mart but because you have helped build a great company the whole town can be proud of? Or are you going to walk around in shame because you embarrassed your kids and neighbors by publicly screwing up your second chance? Your name is on this. Not mine, I'll be gone. But you'll be here and it will either hang around your neck or be a crown on your head. You have to decide. It's your responsibility and you have to ask yourself what you're going to do with your second chance?

One hundred percent to their credit (not my speech), that mill is now profitable and self-funding tens of millions of dollars in capital investments. They are truly creating something special up there, and I'm thrilled to have been able to play a role.

Sacrificial Lamb

It is turnaround doctrine that there must be sacrificial lambs to make it clear that change has begun. In fact the professional certification exam for the Certified Turnaround Professional designation, administered through the Turnaround Management Association includes questions on the value and need of sacrificial lambs. More practically, mistakes have been made and people want justice. Lenders want to see blood, someone needs to pay for putting their money at risk. Vendors and customers want to see justice, and employees are upset that their jobs have been put at risk. In fact, employees will usually tell you who needs to be shown the door. When eight people tell you it's the same person pulling them down they're probably right.

The best thing about sacrificial lambs is that they usually volunteer. There is always some knucklehead who is slow to pick up on the concept of a new sheriff. Sometimes it's the guy who says; "that's not my job" or the fella who refuses to hustle when we clearly need extra effort. Once I caught someone sleeping, so I took a photo and texted it to his union boss before waking him up. Another time I was at a factory with no controls on overtime. It was so bad that one guy had milked only 20 hours of legitimate work into a 70-hour workweek, for years. I declared an end to unauthorized overtime. I'm happy to authorize overtime, just help me understand why it's needed. In one department the guys managed two machines each, but one of them refused to start his second machine that day. When asked by his supervisor he responded; "If I'm not getting overtime anymore then I'm only running one machine." His supervisor was stumped at this logic. So he asked his manager who was also flummoxed. They then came to me. Meanwhile I'm white-knuckled trying to keep the business afloat. I said very simply, "Have him come in here and explain this to me so I can fire him on the spot in front of the whole office and everyone can see how serious I am about saving this business." They went back and delivered my invitation; he chose to start the second machine. Word flew through the factory and I had the benefit of a sacrificial lamb without even firing someone.

When laws have been broken, the guilty person must become the sacrificial lamb. If the CFO has falsified the borrowing base certificate (felony bank fraud), he has to be fired immediately and it has to be explained to the bank. If there are thefts or falsified records (say environmental compliance or safety), they must be fired immediately. This sends a message, but it also protects the business and insulates management from being mistaken as co-conspirators.

Crisis leadership is absorbing the initial shock and keeping everyone focused on their jobs; the bank needs to lend, the workers need to work, the customers need to buy.

If everyone does what they're supposed to do, then the turnaround can work. But we need to get everyone through the turmoil, establish complete control and buy time to address the core issues. Crisis leadership is largely psychological work, and it takes a certain temperament. Once you can get the people doing what needs to be done, the rest of the turnaround is more mechanical.

Chapter 3

Controlling Cash

et's say you've got a great company with solid revenues and reliable profits. Everything is just grand: you're paying all your bills on time, reinvesting in the business, and able to maintain a nice cash reserve. Then things get better. Years of hard work have netted you that one big customer. Bookings and shipments jump 30% and you're scrambling to ramp up. You've got that big surge of adrenaline going. You've finally hooked the white whale you've been chasing for years.

Your bank line of credit helps fund the business's growth as you're ramping up inventory purchases, adding payroll, enduring learning curves and high scrap rates, and adjusting to new equipment. It's all working as expected: the customer keeps consuming your product and ordering more. Fortunes surely await you at the end of this journey, as long as you can continue paying your bills. Then something happens: the new customer pays more slowly, an old customer withholds payment over a quality issue, a critical piece of equipment breaks.

Cash gets tight but you've got a great and growing business so you go see about a bridge loan or some temporary accommodation to help you get through this 60- to 90-day cash shortfall. Your bank is cold to the idea and having second thoughts about what you've done with the money they already lent you. You've maxed out your lines of credit and your other assets are already collateralized. You and your business have taken on the smell of risk and the bank may just slow way down and watch you bleed out. Cash is running out and you're speeding toward a crossroad.

You're in a cash crisis! You're also in the zone of insolvency, which means that management's legal obligations just expanded from the benefit of shareholders and the company to include that of creditors. The zone of insolvency is a gray area, and it is called a zone because a troubled business will likely bump in and out of insolvency based on the formal definitions. Companies can be deemed insolvent in one of two ways: cash-flow insolvency, in which the business lacks the ability to pay its obligations on time, or balance sheet insolvency, in which liabilities are greater than assets.

I point this out because it is a natural reaction of management to take corporate risks to save the business and continue its employment. Although creditors may maximally benefit from a sale or liquidation today, management will want to delay for months of last-ditch efforts. Of course, that risk is how companies are saved, which allows the highest possible recovery, so the zone is a tricky dance of limiting legal exposures and doing what's best for creditors. Courts will look at when management saw the warning signs and acted appropriately. Boards are wise to contact a restructuring attorney or consultant early and carefully document how decisions were made in light of their fiduciary obligation to creditors.

You'll need to convert your financial management from a focus on gross profits to a focus on free cash flow. The first step you need to take is build out a *13-week cash flow forecast* because it is *the* tool by which you will manage your business for the foreseeable future. The 13-week cash-flow forecast tells you when and how you're going to run out of money, and then you must change the circumstances to avoid that fate. In the critical stages of a turnaround, it's a dynamic document that my chief financial officer and I will likely be updating and altering twice a day. Once the business has become predictable, we will do one big update weekly. The key is that the information is updated at least weekly and another week of forecast is added in the future. Although the standard is 13 weeks (one quarter of the year), the models often look out much deeper into the future, usually converting to monthly and quarterly snapshots out 12 months.

When a company is in distress, the consultants, bankers, lawyers, and accountants all immediately shift to the cash flow forecast to manage the business. However, the cash flow forecast model is rarely if ever even discussed in MBA programs. Despite that shortcoming, the 13-week cash-flow forecast is the number-one tool of the insolvency, corporate revitalization, and bankruptcy industry (see Figure 3.1).

13WCFF BORROWING BASE	Week 1 Actual	Week 2 Actual	Week 3 Actual	Week 4 Actual	Week 5 Actual	Week 6 Actual	Week 7 Actual	Week 8 Actual	Week 9 Actual	Week 10 Actual	Week 11 Forecast	Week 12 Forecast	Week 13 Forecast
Beginning AR,gross	$ 583,544	$ 602,473	$ 634,042	$ 532,898	$ 526,116	$ 500,771	$ 608,363	$ 498,635	$ 496,662	$ 430,729	$ 373,046	$ 421,046	$ 522,903
Plus: Billings, net	236,992	171,265	193,215	175,631	201,155	208,429	97,932	229,922	124,143	174,001	200,000	228,000	240,000
Less: Collections	216,063	139,696	294,359	182,413	226,500	100,837	204,653	231,268	189,266	231,169	150,000	124,143	174,001
Less: Discounts	2,000	2,000	254	956	649	422	3,007	627	810	515	2,000	2,000	2,000
Ending AR, net	602,473	634,042	532,898	526,116	500,771	608,363	498,635	496,662	430,719	373,046	421,046	522,903	586,902
Advance rate, net	80%	80%	80%	80%	80%	80%	80%	80%	80%	80%	80%	80%	80%
Advance on AR	$ 481,978	$ 507,234	$ 426,318	$ 420,893	$ 400,617	$ 486,690	$ 398,908	$ 397,330	$ 344,583	$ 298,437	$ 336,837	$ 418,322	$ 469,522
Inventory Value	$ 5,327,842	$ 5,353,403	$ 5,306,354	$ 5,393,473	$ 5,375,988	$ 5,400,149	$ 5,381,700	$ 5,378,439	$ 5,354,165	$ 5,334,528	$ 5,348,428	$ 5,375,085	$ 5,386,785
Advance rate, net	50%	50%	50%	50%	50%	50%	50%	50%	50%	50%	50%	50%	50%
Advnc on Inv ($1.3M cap)	1,300,000	1,300,000	1,300,000	1,300,000	1,300,000	1,300,000	1,300,000	1,300,000	1,300,000	1,300,000	1,300,000	1,300,000	1,300,000
Total Available LOC	$ 1,781,978	$ 1,807,234	$ 1,726,318	$ 1,720,893	$ 1,700,617	$ 1,786,690	$ 1,698,908	$ 1,697,330	$ 1,644,583	$ 1,598,437	$ 1,636,837	$ 1,718,322	$ 1,769,522
Ending LOC Balance	$ 3,000,000	$ 3,000,000	$ 3,000,000	$ 3,000,000	$ 3,000,000	$ 3,000,000	$ 3,000,000	$ 3,000,000	$ 3,000,000	$ 3,000,000	$ 3,000,000	$ 3,000,000	$ 3,000,000
Over (under) formula	$ (1,218,022)	$ (1,192,766)	$ (1,273,682)	$ (1,279,107)	$ (1,299,383)	$ (1,213,310)	$ (1,301,092)	$ (1,302,670)	$ (1,355,417)	$ (1,401,563)	$ (1,363,163)	$ (1,281,678)	$ (1,230,478)

Figure 3.1 13-week cash flow forecast.

DISBURSEMENTS	Week 1	Week 2	Week 3	Week 4	Week 5	Week 6	Week 7	Week 8	Week 9	Week 10	Week 11	Week 12	Week 13
Payroll	103,331	90,544	94,017	79,513	71,825	72,197	69,442	66,899	64,997	63,449	63,000	63,000	63,000
401K	2,920	2,660	2,498	2,348	2,219	2,299	2,276	2,163	1,970	1,957	2,500	2,500	2,500
Health Ins	-	-					12,000	14,592	14,377	13,545	12,000	12,000	12,000
Insurance		16,878			25,469	33,420				47,607			
Rent (don't pay)				573		33,579							
Utility (Power/Sewer)										9,145	4,500	4,500	5,000
P & I - Bank				8,467				8,467				8,467	4,500
Telephone	190	153					777		443	452	1,400		
Shipping & Packaging		1,692		4,036	2,519	2,590		9,187	1,372	4,815	4,500	4,500	4,500
Sales - Travel - Marketing			1,000	1,000	1,000	1,000	1,000	1,000	500	500	500	500	500
Vendor hostage payments		20,000		20,000	3,000		2,000		10,000				
Repairs & Maint					473	4,228		1,763	1,835	369	3,000	3,000	3,000
Cutting Tools		9,040	3,431	1,050	7,549	1,010	2,153	3,873	9,727	3,545	5,000	5,000	5,000
Supplies mfg		5,382			607		3,367	3,679	2,375	4,718	1,000	1,000	1,000
Outside Services	4,006	12,183	11,342	8,596	3,969	24,434	11,800	9,033	6,749	25,531	15,000	15,000	15,000
Direct Material		14,484	1,711	8,184	24,949	8,319	10,314	24,436	6,258	5,148	20,000	20,000	20,000
Castings		13,640		101,209				12,580			5,000	10,000	10,000
Misc	190	110	2,498	925	2,050	2,998	3,180	1,363	1,746	3,378	10,000	10,000	10,000
TOTAL DISBURSEMENTS	110,637	186,766	116,497	235,901	145,629	186,074	118,309	159,036	122,349	184,158	147,400	159,467	156,000
NET CASH	105,426	(47,070)	177,862	(53,488)	80,871	(85,237)	86,344	72,232	66,917	47,011	2,600	(35,324)	18,001
BEGINNING CASH BALANCE		105,426	58,356	236,218	182,730	263,601	178,364	264,708	336,940	403,857	450,868	453,468	418,144
ENDING CASH BALANCE	$ 105,426	$ 58,356	$ 236,218	$ 182,730	$ 263,601	$ 178,364	$ 264,708	$ 336,940	$ 403,857	$ 450,868	$ 453,468	$ 418,144	$ 436,145

Figure 3.1 (Continued)

79

Generate Cash

So you're out of cash and if you're lucky, you'll be forced to fix your problems at their core. You want more cash like a drug addict wants drugs, but a huge pile of cash for you now would just enable more bad behavior. It's time to wake up early, drink a glass of raw eggs, and enforce healthy habits like a longshot Hollywood boxer (remember *Rocky*).

Like the 13-week cash-flow forecast, no one is taught to run a business on cash, and much of it is counterintuitive to what is taught in business school. Recently I was working with a highly competent controller and chief financial officer; both were CPAs and completely thrown off-balance by the idea of managing the business for cash. They had worked mostly within large corporations and never had to worry about cash, so it was a learning experience. With practice, managing cash eventually feels natural. Not only is it critical to survival of the business, managing cash flow can become a fascinating puzzle that really teaches you the balance sheet.

The Four-Legged Stool

A mentor once told me that a healthy and sustainable company must be equally balanced to the benefit of employees, customers, vendors, and ownership, and that when a company is distressed there is an imbalance. Likely, three of the four stakeholder groups have benefited unfairly and to the detriment of one. For most companies that I consult, if you look back over the prior three years, you'll find that the employees have been paid on time, in full, every week.

You'll see that customers have received quality products and below-market prices for a very long time, and that vendors who may now be stretched an extra month or two have enjoyed the past many years being paid on time and in full. But the business is losing money on a broken model and only one party is suffering the pain – namely, the owner and his personally guaranteed debt. The business has to be fixed and made profitable again, but things also need to be rebalanced. Employee accountability needs to increase, more competitive purchasing needs to take place, and prices should be increased. Although I discuss various tactics later, the balanced and healthy business structure is what we're really looking for.

30 Clever Ways to Generate Cash

The most critical skill in growing or fixing a business is the ability to generate cash. Everyone knows how to produce profits (push gross margins up or costs down) but controlling cash is not always the same. New sales with a long cash cycle may improve profits, but it's going to consume rather than generate cash early on. The same is true with any investment in inventory, equipment, or people. As you'll see, the suggestions that follow range from the banal to the extreme, with some defying every sensible business and financial convention in order to stay alive.

1. Raise prices. 100% of business owners agree, "I can't raise prices," and they are 100% incorrect. Years ago I was working with a large regional trucking company and they knew exactly all the reasons they couldn't raise prices: it's a commodity, competitors are in and out of our customer's facility every day, the entire industry is cutting prices and that's the only way to keep business, and so on. Instead, we (mostly one of the owners) put together a brilliant plan to move prices up on customers one by one; we targeted what business we wanted to chase away and what business we had to keep. Net result was that billings increased 15% on similar volume.

If you're in a cash crisis, you can raise prices today and make the increase retroactive to all open invoices. So, you have 30 days payables of $10 million and you just raised prices on past shipments 10%, you've got another $1 million coming your way. Yes, it greatly annoys your customers and you have no legal ground to do this, but this is about your survival not their good tidings. Let's be honest about what is happening here; you're sacrificing future business to preserve the present, and that's the risk you're taking. If you have a technically engineered product, like part of a car or airplane, it might take the customer six months to re-source you and get the product made elsewhere, so the magic balancing formula is this: Can you extract enough cash today to still be in business three months from now, which will generate enough cash to fund a major retention campaign targeting your customer? I've both succeeded and failed with this approach, but it was the three-month business results that determined my success or failure, not how deeply I sliced on the first day.

2. Collect faster. Speeding up collections is your easiest way to get available cash when you need it. You just change your credit terms for new customers and somehow tell all the existing ones that they need to pay faster. Start with your best customer; they are most likely to help. You can offer cash discounts to get paid faster but you shouldn't have to with most customers. Your 13-week cash flow will help you make these decisions. If you're not in crisis, you can subtly work your way toward faster collections without worrying your customers. In crisis phase you do everything possible to shield your customers from your problems, but sometimes you can't fund the business without them. Industries with long program or platform lifecycles like aerospace, pharma and auto get very agitated when you exhibit financial weakness. At the same time, they will support you in a moment of crisis, if compelled. A big retailer is likely just to dump you and your products if you exhibit weakness.

3. Collect now. An even better way to generate cash and annoy customers is to ask for payment immediately. For example, "Shipments have been halted, all bills are due today and all future payment terms will be COD." The business is going anaerobic (the body consumes itself for survival) and your bet is you can get things turned around fast enough to hold it all together. Part of this tactic is knowing your leverage. For example, if you make a tiny little part on a car, your failure to ship could stop an entire assembly line, which makes your survival very important and the auto makers will support you if needed (until they replace you). If you make and sell decorative pillows to gift shops, you have very little leverage, and your customers don't even have to acknowledge your new terms, let alone adhere to them.

4. Slow payables. Years ago a local bank called me to help out some wonderful and endearing entrepreneurs who were always struggling with cash. It seemed like once a month they would need a bank overadvance. The company had both an ambulance service and funeral home (yes, a vertically integrated business) and seemed to range between having +7 to −3 days of cash on hand at any given time. We methodically worked with vendors to extend payment terms one week, which increased our on-hand cash range from +14 to +4 days. Faster collections got us another week (+21 to +11 days) and with no changes to the business they were now safely operating with a cash cushion and no longer upsetting their lender.

A more radical approach occurred with a trucking company. Their bank declared it was time for liquidation and refused to fund any payments "until you can present us with a plan that the bank can support." The trucking company hoarded cash and didn't pay anyone, and a week later it had been shut-off from the bulk diesel market and it was receiving angry vendor calls, but it had accumulated $1,000,000 in cash. Now they had cash to work with and they had just swapped the insufferable pain caused by a hostile senior secured creditor for the annoying but relatively harmless pain of everyone else – and they had picked up a million dollars in the trade. They built from there, got everyone paid in full eventually and saved over 600 jobs in the process.

My father always paid his vendors a few days early and took pride in wanting to be their best customer. For decades he told me that he was building good will when he could afford it, just in case he ever needed their help in bad times. When his turnaround happened, he got immediate 75-day terms from his core vendors because he had built up that good will over many years.

5. Formalize procurement. This means issuing a memo that all purchases over $1,000 require a purchase order (PO), and all purchase orders over maybe $5,000 must have CEO approval. Invoices will not be paid unless they are supported by these purchase orders. Often in turnarounds, the accounting department is squeezing pennies while the purchasing department just keeps issuing POs. You can start by approving all purchases in the next 30 or 60 days then just raising the approval threshold as things settle down.

6. Sell equipment. If you have idle equipment, it's time to sell it. You're no longer in the capacity game, you're in the survival game. Call the auctioneer or post it on eBay and turn it into cash. If the bank has a lien on it, then talk to them and work out a deal where you can keep some of the money. When I have a current appraisal, I might be able to convince the bank to keep the forced liquidation value (FLV, also known as auction value) and let the company keep any premium above FLV. If nothing else, selling equipment makes the bank happy, pays down debt, and is symbolic of a company's commitment to making the business lean.

7. Sell inventory. When selling inventory, the first step is an inventory audit and categorization into four buckets:

a. Old dead inventory.

b. Old but active inventory.

c. New, slow-moving inventory.

d. New, quick-moving inventory.

The old-dead stuff hasn't moved in 12 or 18+ months. You're looking to identify inventory that no longer provides value to you. Use common sense; a critical spare part is not what we're looking to get rid of here. We just want old, dead inventory that can be gotten rid of in one of several ways: repurpose, refashion, fire sale, or scrap. You're going to take a dead item and extract cash from it very quickly. This will hurt your income statement and your (inflated) balance sheet, but maybe 10% of that loss will become positive cash in the business and it will feel like a great bargain to you.

Repurposing might be converting a container of broom poles into flag poles or turning rolls of carpet into door mats. Refashioning might be repainting to a better color or swapping out the lampshades on a popular base. Fire selling is selling off a large volume at a steep discount to customers or liquidators and, of course, scrap is simply that; pennies on the dollar in recovery.

One caveat to selling off inventory for a cash-strapped company where there is an obstacle is when you have borrowed against it already. A typical manufacturing situation is that the company has a revolving line of credit which advances 85% on receivables and 50% on inventory. The company's borrowing base or head-room expands as inventory values expand so there is a perverse incentive that allows inventory values to be "rounded up" over time. Scrapping $1 million of inventory for $100,000 in cash makes sense in a pinch but it will reduce your borrowing availability by $500,000 and likely exacerbate issues with your lender. This can all be worked through but you should secure lender support while you monetize the balance sheet.

The "old but active" inventory just needs to be leaned out. Figure out what your near-term need will be and move the rest to customers with discount programs or dump it to a discount retailer.

The real-value opportunity in inventory is through creative thinking and analysis. The next easiest target is slow-moving younger inventory. This is stuff that's overstocked and will become old, dead inventory over time. You've got to lean this out and get it to turnover more quickly. Distributors do it all the time, offering specials on overstocks on old inventory.

The next step involves a joint exercise between your marketing, inventory, and finance departments. SKUs are stock-keeping units or individual inventory types; it's how we keep track of inventory, and product companies usually have too many. Do you really need to sell 31 flavors when 80% of your sales come from only 5 flavors? Couldn't you sell that same 80% with only 25 or even 20 flavors? The Pareto Principle (80/20 Rule) is universal, so just on math alone you should always be trimming some of your offerings. That excess is soaking up inventory dollars and also time and resources throughout your business. SKU rationalization is best done thoughtfully, but big, quick, instinctive changes usually work just fine.

8. Default on all debt. It's a prelude to any debt restructuring and it uses a company's money to fund its recovery. Now, every bank is different; some will drain you of cash through default rates of interest and fees like overdraft, forbearance fees, and a much larger loan-modification fee. Other lenders will protect the business and allow what precious little cash they do have to be recirculated in the business. Either way, stop paying any of your debt and let your cash accumulate. You need to keep the cash in the business. This will likely get you moved to the workout department, but that's where you want to end up since these are the people authorized to discount and restructure debts. It's a risky move, so make sure you know what you're doing and anticipate your lender's next move. See Chapter 4 for more on dealing with your bank.

A recent European client had a fast growing and profitable business that was largely wrapped up in the founder's ego. He accelerated his global expansion and decided to build a fancy new building (monument) as the company headquarters, both of which led to a severe cash drain. The banks balked at his aggressive plans and he was insulted. He felt it was a direct insult to him personally (it wasn't) and to his business acumen (it was). To show them what an honorable man of character he was, he took all his available cash and paid down the bank. "That should show them," he said. "They question my ability to pay and I show them to their face that I can pay my bills!" "Yes," I replied, "but now you're broke, the construction of your new building is stalled, your supply chain is backing up, and you're in crisis." Had he held on to his money, taken a hit to his ego, annoyed the banks, and kept the supply chain intact, he'd have leverage and a healthier business. Instead, he gave away all his leverage and cash and now had nothing but his ego. PS: A fancy new headquarters building is almost always a bad idea.

9. Layoffs. The U.S. economy embraces the concepts of renewal and creative destruction. We have hope that every time a door closes, a new door will open and because of that, workers are free to leave jobs without future obligation and employers are free to cut jobs without future obligation. This means that in the United States you can often lay off people with minimal severance cost (see the WARN Act discussion in Chapter 6) so the cash benefit to the company is often immediate. In Mexico, Canada, and Europe, from what I've seen, severance is often 3 to 24 months' worth of wages, meaning that there is no cash return on investment (ROI) on layoffs and it's actually a cash drain on distressed businesses. So instead of saving the body with an amputation, the entire workforce stays employed, driving the insolvency deeper. When layoffs can generate cash, do them. Go deep and quick with your cuts, then focus on recovery with the survivors. It's far better to do one deep cut than several small middling ones that lack courage. Most beleaguered entrepreneurs later admit that the first layoff was actually easy and a good thing, they cut redundancies and a few bad actors. It's the second and third round of layoffs that really hurt. Consider reduced hours in lieu of a second or third round of layoffs. Some states like New York have workshare programs which allow employees to collect unemployment benefits for those days not worked. European companies often have similar programs and backfill those lost wages with social payments.

10. Reduce wages. In 2009 many companies cut employee wages to cut costs and generate cash. Properly motivated, most people will sacrifice for the common good. Now they must be motivated and need to feel that their common sacrifice really does benefit the common good because they have to go home and explain to their spouse why this pay cut makes sense and why they're willing to stick it out for the team.

Nothing will create ill will faster than sending a valued employee home to explain his 10% wage cut only to come back and see the CEO acting like an entitled jerk. Mac, an entrepreneur, slashed wages and months later had his new $70,000 sauna delivered to the warehouse before having it delivered to his lake house in the company truck. Tim was so obtuse that he waited less than one month after slashing employee wages before he moved his racing Porsche into the warehouse for winter storage. One entrepreneur's wife made her sacrifice visible by moving from a Mercedes sedan to a Porsche 911. She told us twice of her sacrifice, as if we missed the point the first time. As an entrepreneur and a leader, you (and your family) are expected to suffer first and suffer most when times get tough. That means the first person to work extra hours, sacrifice vacations, and take the first pay cut is the CEO. We all know this intuitively, but it takes tremendous courage, and too often CEOs want to preserve their lifestyle at whatever cost others must endure.

11. Restart credit plans. If I'm attempting to restart a factory without any cash I can go to the vendors (who are all owed a bunch of money by the prior owner) and convince them to fund our restart. It's in their best interest to save a customer and improve their odds of recovery on old debt. My pitch is that I need to freeze all past-due balances immediately and I also need 90-day credit terms and an open credit limit, because I'm ready to order a bunch of material to restart the factory. Let's say my factory ships $10 million per month with a 40% material cost, and I'm looking for 90 days of restart credit. That's $4 million in material purchases monthly, so I'm seeking $12 million total credit.

This is the intellectual riddle I love so much about turnarounds, I'm trying to restart a factory and put 500 people to work, but I've got the world's worst poker hand. The balance sheet is shot, the company stalled out, the supply chain is locked up, lawsuits are everywhere, employees are vanishing, and so are customers – but I think we can put the company back on track again, with none of our own cash. The first thing we need is leverage; I get the senior secured lender to let me produce the backlog in exchange for some debt reduction to them. Then I stop everyone in their tracks with the announcement that the bank will support the restart if, and only if, the stakeholder parties support and work within the confines of our plan. With bank support, everyone now wants to talk and hear our plan. Knowing the vendors are upset and unlikely to unanimously support my $12 million credit plan, our attorney crafts a special debt treatment where participating vendors are granted an improved position in the debt stack. Vendors then self-select whether they will keep us as a customer and recover old debts through an improved position or will they opt to lose a customer and come up short in recovery? The vendors who choose to be supportive get our devotion and are a priority repayment. Now we have a plan that makes sense, has multiple leverage points, and is likely to be supported.

No doubt these restart credit plans are tough coalitions to build and hold, but you are doing virtuous work, so despite the odds, good fortune is on your side.

12. Vendor negotiations. Over the years I've personally negotiated with thousands of vendors and every single conversation starts with the vendor saying something like; "You're cut off until we get paid," which is reasonable but misses the point. What they really want is security of payment and continued profits. I respond with something along the lines of the following:

> I will get you paid but let's review for a minute. From my calculations you have made 10 to 20 times that amount in gross profits on our business over the years, so your risk is either a small haircut or you can recoup that amount plus another 10 to 20 times into the future. I'm being totally upfront with you, we have a 90-day cash need and we are reevaluating our entire supply chain. Future vendors are being selected based on their willingness to help us through this need. If you commit to 90-day terms now, you will be our future vendor and we will repay your help with profits and loyalty. If not, I am forced to shop the business elsewhere.

If we need to pay cash to someone else for an order or two, just to make Supplier 1 panic, we will. Again, we're creating leverage from thin air.

The next level of vendor negotiations leans on psychological tactics such as the following:

- **Fear of missing out.** Our vendors stay with us for years and decades, so are you willing to be locked out of this company for 10 years based on 90 days of credit? Does the vice president of sales support that decision?

- **Fear of nonconformance.** You are the only one who is acting in this extreme and punitive manner. Everyone else wants to support and share in our future success. Even the governor of the state has publicly supported our plan – but you are fighting it. What is motivating you to act this way?

- **Fear of employment 1.** Perhaps it's better not to take the risk of being hung with this decision, maybe we should talk to your boss?

o **Fear of employment 2.** Are you authorized to write down debt for the corporation? Are you authorized to turn down 10 years of future business? When this call ends I will send a letter to your president either praising you or detailing what I feel is your myopic point of view. Before you do yourself any harm, why don't you just pass me on to your boss?

If you can't get even 30 days out of the gate, propose an expanding payment term arrangement:

o On delivery for first one or two orders

o 15 days for the next order

o 30 days thereafter

13. Debt for credit swaps. Occasionally there is a recalcitrant vendor who is irreplaceable and has absolute leverage over your business. If they support you the business will survive. If not, it won't. They can afford the 90-day terms but they want to extract more money in the deal. I've been forced to sweeten the offer with long-term debt on our balance sheet in exchange for near-term credit. When you are out of options, it seems reasonable to accrue a 10% premium on all purchases for a year with a long-term payback schedule.

For example, let's say I need to order $100,000 from you monthly and I need 90-day payment terms to fund my restart. This means I need $300,000 in vendor credit from you (3 months of $100,000 per month). To compensate you for this extension of credit, I will pay you on time at the 90 days and will also accrue an extra 10% premium on my purchases. This accrued balance will sit on my balance sheet as long-term debt. So, every month I order $100,000 in product from you and I accrue 10% of that purchase (10% of $100,000 monthly = $10,000/month = $120,000/year). This premium payment incentivizes you to support us with healthy credit terms during our first year back in business. It's a great deal for you; at the end of one year, you'll have sold $1.2 million of product to a devoted customer. You'll also have earned an additional $120,000 for the extension of $300,000 in payment terms.

For you, the entrepreneur, it's a lousy deal, because you're paying full price plus a 10% premium. The benefit is it helps us build cash flow of the business. We are paying $120,000 (slowly, over time) to borrow $300,000 today, which allows us to revive a business with little of our own cash. It is an unsecured liability that participates in the risk of the business. We can also raise our prices to recoup this expense.

In really tough situations, I've been forced to accept 100% of my request in new long-term debts. That's in addition to the old debts that are already owed. So let's say, using the same example as previously, that I request 90 days, which is $300,000 in vendor credit, and you are such a heartless bastard that you force me to immediately sign an additional $300,000 note for security and your long-term (unscrupulous) profits. Yes, I paid that once. Without regrets.

14. Debt for equity. Similar to point 13, we're selling our plan for the future in exchange for our stakeholders' financial support, and if we do a great job it's only natural for them to want an actual stake in our future success. So, for $300,000 in trade credit to the right vendor, I might be willing to offer $300,000 in future-value equity. The key here is future value. Maybe you pick three years out, do your projections, and figure out what percentage of ownership now might be worth $300,000 then. If they provide critical support and you hit your numbers, why not? Only an entrepreneurial vendor/partner will take you up on this, and they could be a huge help to you in many ways over the years.

Many business owners are hung up on retaining 100% equity, but I'm not so much. I'd rather have more partners across more businesses than all my eggs in one isolated basket. Others are, understandably, hung up on maintaining majority control, but I've loosened on that opinion over the years because I've better understood the protections good corporate governance can offer minority shareholders.

15. Factoring. Factoring is a way to quickly leverage a business's accounts receivable. Most turnarounds I'm brought into have already leveraged accounts receivable to the hilt, so factoring offers no additional benefit. But, in a buyout or acquisition, it works wonders. Factoring is also quick and can often be put in place within two weeks, whereas a finance company asset-based line of credit (ABL LOC) might take four weeks, and a bank will be two months or a quick refusal.

There are two types of factoring: (1) recourse, where if the customer doesn't pay the invoice, the factor can come back to you for the money. (2) Nonrecourse where the factor "buys" the receivable from you and it's 100% their responsibility to collect.

16. Purchase order financing. This works great for importers who deal in finished goods that can be easily liquidated. If we get a purchase order (PO, a binding contract that entices me to spend money producing their product for specified payment) from a big national retailer that I'm going to have produced in China and delivered to the customer in the United States, then I can likely finance the whole order using PO financing. I'll take my PO to a PO financer who will issue me a term sheet describing how they will take ownership of the finished product at the port in China and hold ownership of the product on its voyage across the ocean. The Chinese manufacturer feels secure because they'll be paid in full at the port. The lender feels secure because they will control the product (which has a binding PO) during the entire length of their involvement. As an entrepreneur, I love it because no cash ever came out of my pocket to fund the order but I still control the largest portion of proceeds from the sale.

For the most part, PO financing only works with finished goods (which can be seized and quickly liquidated by the lender) and does not work for products that transition from raw materials to finished goods under your ownership (as in your factory). It is very hard to find a lender who will PO finance orders produced in a U.S. factory for delivery to a customer within the United States. The explanation is that, if something goes wrong, the PO lender can't come into my factory and recover their money from a pile of half-built parts. But if something goes wrong on an import order, they just divert the container to the customer or a liquidator.

17. Pre-invoice UCC filing. I've used this clever method to fund a domestic factory order when PO financing couldn't. We went to the manufacturer and showed it both our PO from a national retailer along with our proforma invoice that we would present to the retailer when shipment was made against the PO. We then filled out a Uniform Commercial

Code UCC-1 lien for the producer, giving the producer a lien on our future invoice, which would guarantee the producer payment from the retailer. If distrust or distress is high, an escrow agent can be used to receive and disburse funds from the retailer. Lenders often issue comfort letters to provide assurances that obligations will be met. Since the lender is usually controlling cash at this point, the lender can promise to segregate that invoice payment and remit it to the supplier. This induces the supplier to help and provides comfort and explanation to the supplier's own bank.

Let me illustrate how this works; we receive a $1 million purchase order from Big Box Retailer that has a 40% gross profit margin for us (I will spend $600,000 to have it produced and will keep $400,000 in gross profit for my part as designer, broker, and salesman) and 30-day payment terms. I show my vendor (the factory owner who doesn't have a relationship with my customer) both the customer's PO and my proforma invoice. Then we both fill out the UCC-1 and the vendor files it with the Secretary of State or at the courthouse. The factory owner now has a priority legal claim of $600,000 on my $1 million invoice. With that security, he buys materials, assembles labor, and produces the goods. He then ships to the retailer and waits 30 days for payment. Big Box Retailer receives the goods along with my invoice. As obligated, Big Box Retailer pays the invoice in full 30 days after receipt. We split the proceeds as agreed, I get $400,000 and the factory owner gets $600,000. We all win through the magic of creative finance; the retailer got the product it wanted, the factory got the order it wanted, and I made my share, all with no financial exposure.

18. Vendors place inventory on consignment. In this situation we get the vendors to place their inventory on our shelves, but they maintain ownership interest. This way we (the customer) have stocked shelves but the vendor maintains title over the goods as opposed to selling the product on open-payment terms and being way down in the general unsecured creditor stack. When the product is sold, the vendor receives payment and releases title to the goods. The recent Sports Authority bankruptcy case has changed this long-standing method, because secured creditors have been able to claim title to the consigned goods.

19. Vendor sells inventory on terms and files a UCC lien against that inventory until they are paid. Here the vendor delivers goods and files a UCC lien against those specific inventory assets. This works when there are no prior inventory liens (unlikely) or when the secured creditor allows the vendor first position on those inventory assets, which might happen if the items are of critical importance to the turnaround plan.

20. Vendor holds a dated check. We ask the vendor to let us pay by check, but they hold the check for X days. (It is a crime and personal liability to send a bad check in the United States, so that's their assurance that we are not playing games). Sometimes a series of dated checks will provide comfort to a vendor.

21. Cash from your customers.
"You're going to shut down the (Big 3 auto) factory!" screamed the buyer.
"Yeah, I know," I responded calmly.

"You know! You're going to know very well because the penalty is $250,000 per hour if we're line-down," he screamed. No kidding, the penalties really are that steep.

"I know, that's a lot of money. I bet it could cost even more than that."

"You're damn right it's more than that, it's going to cost you a fortune – so what are you going to do about it?"

"Well, there's just not much I can do about it, we're out of money."

[Long and Awkward Silence]

"Well, how much do you need?" was his pained response.

At the end of our pleasant conversation I had the cash I needed to get our factory moving again.

22. Cash value of life insurance. Life insurance is often one of an entrepreneur's smartest investments. The money can go in pretax and protects the company (and heirs) from the sudden loss of its founder or a key person. This is called "key-man" life insurance and your bank wants you to have it. So you take out a large key-man whole life insurance policy, fund it from the company and build up a significant cash value. The investment <u>may</u> be considered an exempt asset and protected in bankruptcy. Additionally, life insurance expense is often buried in the income statement amidst all the other corporate insurance expenses so it's never obvious how much you're socking away from the company for your benefit. In a turnaround, you can either just keep quiet about your large and protected cash balance (and keep funding it) or you can borrow or use that cash balance to help fund the company turnaround. Consult a lawyer.

23. Subleasing parts of your business. This is the famous Arnold Goldstein example of the restaurant owner who leased out the valet parking concession to a private company. So the valet company paid the restaurant for the privilege of operating at his location. Another example was a distributor of consumer goods who found someone that would pay rent and buy broken cases of products to run an off-price store out of the back corner of their warehouse. Now the distributor is getting rental income and full recovery on damaged inventory.

24. Sale leaseback. This works well with large assets like a building or a big piece of equipment. Let's say you own your factory, which is appraised for $10 million, but your business is cash poor. To rectify the imbalance, you can sell your building to an investor and at the same time lock in a long-term (say 20 years) lease on the building. This puts $10 million of cash (minus debts, fees, and taxes) in your pocket but increases your monthly breakeven by the amount of the lease. You're losing the value of a real estate investment, but potentially funding the turnaround of your company.

25. S t r e t c h payments. When cash is tight, wait until you get the shutoff notice from your utility companies. They don't have much wiggle room, so be open with them and always get the check there before they mobilize the trucks. I have clients who have existed in this perilous state for years on end. Insurances also have hard cut-offs that you can stretch up against. Taxes may also be stretchable, but I never play games with Caesar.

26. Accelerated tax returns. One client took his business from zero to $45 million in five years, then back to zero in the next five years. On his way up, he was paying taxes on earnings of over $10 million annually; on his way down he was losing millions annually. A big income loss on the heels of big gains can create a future tax refund. Somehow, there was a temporary filing loophole and he got his local congressman to walk his tax return through the IRS, which netted an expedited $1.5 million tax refund, about six months faster and with no audit. By the time Uncle Sam wanted his money back, the cash and the business were both long gone. The IRS has since closed that loophole.

27. Beware unaccrued liabilities. Warranty claims, gift certificates, customer deposits, equipment repairs, insurance renewals, taxes, permits, and fees can all sneak up on you. Think through every single thing and get it on your cash-flow forecast.

28. Delay and stall collections. See Chapter 8, "Debt Restructuring Out of Court." There are myriad tactics that I cover in Chapter 8, but the most important concept is the priority-of-debt rule; if the bank and government are not being paid in full then no vendor debt should be paid at all. That's an oversimplification on my part, but it explains the general theory we are working under. Don't give collectors empty promises or apologies; just explain the situation and how their claims will be handled.

29. *Never, ever, ever* skip tax withholdings. Ever! See Chapter 6, "Arsonists and Regulators." Trustees and trust accounts are held to the very highest legal and fiduciary standards. The safest thing you can do is automate the collection and remittance process with your payroll firm – out of arm's reach.

30. Move the cash. If your bank is hostile and you fear they will sweep all your cash, then you have to protect the business and your cash. The first time I did this, the bank swept our account that night, wondering what happened to the $200,000 that had been there just hours before. It was hysterical that next morning when the bank freaked out, but really scary when we were doing it. Nothing will move a bank into attack mode faster than moving your (their) money to another bank. It's a dicey move. You're protecting yourself but realize that it's gloves off in the morning.

The best way I've found to balance this risk is to move the money away from the bank but to a place that's less offensive than another bank. In one situation, we moved hundreds of thousands of dollars out by prefunding payroll. We moved the money to our payroll service and explained "we feel secure having a month of payroll prepaid in case of a shut-down (oblique threat) and, quite frankly, we weren't sure we could trust you not to sweep it." Prepaying other utility-type expenses, like the electric bill or insurance, are also some-what tolerable to the bank. In my experience, they usually only come for the money once and a successful (noninflam-matory) block will put you in a good position to negotiate cash application on more favorable terms.

Chapter 4

When Banks Attack

Chapter 1

When Sepsis Attack

When a business's results slip and the bank has that first tough conversation with the owner, emotions often surge. The owner's mind swirls into a sea of thoughts which usually follow this arc:

> What the heck, these guys are my buddies, they just recently invited me to their annual golf event last summer – and I even met the local president who was very complimentary of me and my business. There must be a mistake; I've been borrowing money from this bank for 10 years and the people there have always told me I was one of their valued clients. By the way, have you seen the amount of interest I'm paying to those greedy bums annually? They're in the business of lending money; why would they want to limit my ability to borrow now? They knew the risks, etc.

I know, I've been there. One day you're the bank's best friend and the next day you're not. Over the years I've realized that banks really only have two departments: lending and collections, finders and grinders. That guy with the nice suit, expense account, and low golf handicap (your buddy) – he's the finder/lender. The rumpled troll with a sour disposition, no expense account, and no golf game – he's the grinder/collector. Banks develop pleasant euphemisms for the collection department like workout, special assets, and specialized finance, but the jobs are is all the same – to get the bank's money back from you.

During my first turnaround, our banker (Kenny – strong handshake, winning smile, great tan) came in hard and really surprised us. Our rotten CFO was hiding losses with inventory accounting games. In 24 hours, I went through the stages of grief, which included thoughts like: Hey, I thought we were all in this together, they knew the risk they were taking, and so on. Late at night I thought about the loan agreement we had signed, which of course I had never read. I read it that night and realized that banks have been lending money for over 7,000 years and I'd been borrowing for about four at that point. Clearly, I was outgunned. Heck, I'd even signed away my right to a jury trial because big mean banks don't win in front of juries. The next step in my aggressive denial was to contemplate bankruptcy. I got online, looked at the schedules, and realized that in Louisiana (the state where my business and I resided) we would get to keep something like my wife's wedding band, a mattress, one cow, and a handful of chickens. Resolved that I had no good options, I committed myself to learning the turnaround game and fighting my way out of this hole.

While my mind was spinning through that emotional roller coaster, here's what the bank was thinking:

> As a federally insured bank, regulators make us measure and rate all loans with special attention to the poor performers. We don't like the poor performers, nor do we charge enough to absorb the risk of poor performers. We have a fiduciary obligation to our shareholders and depositors to either get these poorly performing credits healthy or move them out of our bank. In the past we've loaned money to deceitful people, and therefore we need to treat all troubled borrowers with the jaundiced eye of suspicion that they might be the next morally deficient borrower we deal with. We need to be firm but pleasant and slowly liquidate this business out from under the entrepreneur.

Yikes!

You're now a topic in credit committee on Monday mornings, and you probably have been for several weeks or months now. The tough conversation you just had with the bank had been coming at you for quite some time, you just didn't realize it. The credit committee wants to know one thing from you: Do you understand the situation and are you committed to the solution? Oh, there are a hundred things on their checklist but first they need to know where your head is. They want to meet in one week and they are going to be looking deep into your eyes to understand your clarity and your commitment. How you respond will be discussed in credit committee next week and your response will determine your future treatment. These relationships can quickly spiral downward if things start off on the wrong foot, like for several of my former clients:

Steve – had a fast-growing and very profitable business that then went into decline. He generally ignored the bank and thought their demands were petty and they didn't appreciate his brilliance. He stopped paying contractors, had trouble shipping orders, but every weekend he still valet-parked his Rolls Royce at the local yacht club (where the top regional bankers were all members). Eventually the bank took a $10 million loss on Steve, while other creditors lost another $6 million.

Floyd – called me to complain about the horrible private equity investors who were ruining his business and doing all sorts of mean-spirited things to him. This, only three months after they had invested $2 million into his business. He and I talked through the weekend and I drove to see him on Monday. After a quick review of his financial statements, I said they just didn't make sense to me, things were not lining up and something was amiss. Common-sense formulas were out of balance. He gave me some weak answers first and then admitted that the numbers were completely made up. Wholly fabricated. Seriously, he said he just made them up, every single one based on an idea of how he thinks the business should look or could look, or something. He must have done a good job because the financials sailed right through a $40,000 quality of earnings review by a well-known regional CPA firm.

Worse yet, he was really upset about the interest rate they were charging him. Our conversation went like this:

> Him: Well yeah, I made it all up but they're charging me 15% interest and that's ridiculous.
>
> Me: But you took the $2 million from them and it's all gone now?
>
> Him: Yes, but 15% is usurious.
>
> Me: But you're not paying the interest. You took $2 million in cash, it's all gone, you haven't made a single payment – and you're complaining about the interest rate?
>
> Him: Yes.

Serge – maxed out his revolving line of credit and with no additional ability to borrow, so he began creating phony invoices, submitted those to the bank and borrowed real money against phony (fraudulent, illegal) invoices. The bank never caught on and he "borrowed" an additional $1 million more than his collateral would support. It wasn't until Serge did something even dumber that an employee contacted the FBI and mentioned the felony bank fraud as an ancillary issue.

Ralph – like Steve but with a Corvette. Ralph had no interest in scaling back his lifestyle. He'd roll into the bank to meet with some midcareer lender making $80,000 a year working long hours to raise a family and Ralph would spend the whole meeting bragging about his sailboat. Before running out of money, Ralph had burned through his last $1 million launching his Asian division – living in Bangkok, without his wife, for a year. (Lots of start-up expense, you know.)

Steve, Floyd, Serge, and Ralph each lost his business. Meanwhile, other entrepreneurs I've worked with each embraced salvation and today each still owns his business.

Want Leverage? Don't Pay the Bank!

There's an old saying: when I owe the bank $1 million, I have a problem. But when I owe the bank $10 million, the bank has a problem. It's counterintuitive, but the bank is less likely to negotiate with you if you're making all your payments in full and on time. No matter what you say, they just want you to keep making payments and improving their position, not yours. Once you stop paying, there is something to talk about and you're likely to be transferred to workout who will work with you.

As much as banks want the CEO to change, they don't want to force progress. And, secretly, they're really afraid of lender liability laws. Yes, lender liability, such as if they take control of your company, make poor decisions, and your business fails. You can sue them for damages, probably a multiple of your prior business's revenue. A few lenders push the envelope with control, but most (99%) are very conservative in their actions. They speak in confusing ways and twist your arm until you give in – "Okay, okay, tell me what to do. I'll do anything to have you fund my payroll on Friday." "Oh, we can't really tell you what to do but you better do something," and they twist your arm further. Sweat is beading on your brow (I know, I've experienced this) and they ask if you've looked at cost reductions? "Yes," you scream and they twist your arm harder. All you can think of is funding payroll and all they can think of is squeezing cash out of you. "Have you considered hiring a turnaround professional?" they ask. You give them a blank stare (like I did) and they hand you my business card.

As in an old western movie, the bank kicks you out the front door back onto the street. You dust yourself off and wander back to the factory, head spinning. The people at the bank gave you my card because you will meet with them again in one week, and they expect you to have complete control of the situation and the business. *This* very moment separates success from failure more than any other moment in the turnaround cycle. Psychologically your primate brain is considering two options: compliance or defiance. You're rattled, but when you imagine it, compliance looks weak and you're not ready for that. You're a proud entrepreneur and not about to kowtow to anyone. Defiance has an emotional appeal, especially for an entrepreneur up against a bunch of bankers. But if you've read this far, you know it's the road to ruin. Compliance is the best solution because it requires the courage and conviction of an entrepreneur along with the clear-eyed commitment of the reformed. Plus, it's the most fun because, if you hit the gas right now, in the right direction, you can pull out of this quickly with very little scar tissue. The beauty of insolvency and distress is that, with ratlike cunning, leverage can be turned quickly.

Think about it, you're up against a bank and the court system. If you take control right now, you can come up with a solid turnaround plan and begin executing it immediately. It's a bank, and people there don't move quickly, so they'll never catch up with you – as long as you're going in the right direction. But if you just sit there, you will get run over. While the bankers are focused elsewhere, you can come up with an idea at 8:00 a.m., cash forecast it by 9:00, start implementing it by noon, and tell your bank the initial results in your weekly recap, which they'll read later. By then you've made 10 other changes and you control momentum.

The next meeting is scheduled in one week and they expect great things from you.

A bank lends money based on certain criteria known as the 5 Cs of credit: character, capacity, capital, collateral, and conditions. They collect on slightly different criteria:

1. **Communication** – If they brought the problem to you, then you have failed this test. They cannot yet rely on you to manage your business and be forthcoming with important information about their money, and this is the foundation of trust. You can rebuild this trust over time.

2. **Character** – Your next move will reveal your character. When they first loaned you the money, they considered

your character and asked around the community about your reputation. Do you pay your bills, have you been sued, how often and for what, are you litigious? And they want to know about you, the borrower, as a businessperson; are you someone who's going nowhere with his business or maybe you've just gotten lucky early in your career, or are you a grizzled veteran with plenty of scar tissue? If so, what's your reputation in dealing with banks? Right now they want a CEO who is competent, trustworthy, and ready to suffer through a turnaround.

3. **Collateral** – The bank has already performed a forced liquidation valuation (FLV) on your business, so they know what the bottom line is. Lenders repeat the old axiom: "Our first loss is our best loss" like a mantra. It is better to pull the plug today and suffer the consequences of liquidation than to risk more capital on a turnaround. That's what you're up against and it takes a stunning level of salesmanship and credibility to persuade the lender to reach deeper into his pocket for your business. If the lender initiated the conversation, then you have lost that credibility, which is why the bank gave you my card.

The bank likely asked you to update your personal financial statement (PFS) for the next meeting. Be careful when filling this out, lenders compare it to your tax returns and if the documents don't agree, then the question is which party you're lying to; the Internal Revenue Service (IRS) or a federally insured bank – both are felonies. Your lender buddies will want to bring dominion over your assets, so expect to re-sign-away your rights and to transfer control of your investment accounts. I recently saw a bank demand the borrower fill out and sign a 40-page Affidavit of Personal Financial Condition, which I suspect was more of a psychological weapon since it already had an updated PFS.

4. **Controls** – How tightly do you run your ship? Are your financial reports accurate and timely? What does your controller's desk look like? A cluttered desk reveals a cluttered mind and is untrustworthy in accounting. If you run your business like a commune and trust employees to always do the right thing, then you're more likely to have environmental, tax, and labor issues. If you run your business like a Navy ship, you're less likely to have these hidden liabilities.

5. **Capital, aka, Skin in the Game** – The bank wants you fully invested and in a position where you absolutely cannot afford to fail. Whereas the bank can afford to take a loss, you cannot. If given the chance, you will find a way to survive. They want you up late worrying about their money.

Although I recommend a strategy of compliance and becoming an A-student when in trouble with the bank, every so often you may have to fight them to save the company. On one of my first turnarounds, I had taken control of a company on Monday, fired the CFO for bank fraud on Tuesday, and had the bank sweep all remaining cash out of our account Tuesday night. Wednesday morning we needed to fund payroll and didn't have a dime to do it. It was day 3 and they had me, checkmate. One hundred people were going to lose their jobs that week. In a panic I called the bank, with nothing but desperation and some trumped up courage. They were ready for me, the two bankers had me on speaker phone so they could giggle at their own snarky replies while I floundered. I led with charm and reason and got nowhere. I could hear their chests puffing as they talked about rights of setoff, blah, blah, blah. They had every single legal right on their side, all I had on my side was 100 families. The conversation dragged on and the odds stacked up against me.

I had nothing left, it was oblivion or I go full commando. I'm not sure what that means, but in my mind, it's the complete and resolute willingness to cause utter chaos and destruction to achieve my goal. If I go down, you're all coming with me. I think that's the level of dedication the employees deserve. I separated who the boss was on our phone call and told her that she needed to make a very clear and very definite decision: would they fund payroll or not? She said, "No." "Let me restate," I said, "you are making one very singular decision that you will own completely, you either keep our money or you fund payroll." Blah, blah, blah was her reply, some explanation about the rights of the bank.

I had one card left; "Your choice, I either tell the employees you supported them or I call the chairman of your bank." "We're not funding payroll," she said. "I'll give you one more chance ..." she cut me off with a snarky, "No."

I hung up and dialed. For the next 5 hours I called every number and emailed every email I could find for this very large bank – a bank that covered about half the United

States and was headquartered 1,200 miles from me. With every single call, I politely asked for the Chairman, by name, and then left the following message: "Unless I get a call back today we are laying off 100 people, shutting the business, and suing your bank for all the damages under lender liability law." If you ever wanted people to both hate you, and return your call, this is the tactic. The next morning I was with a local bank executive who funded payroll. The snarky lender was demoted, then fired, and we got the company turned around. Final tally: the bank was paid 100% in full, every job preserved, and a few feathers ruffled.

Receivership

When trust is lost and the borrower is seen to be destroying value, lenders can have the sheriff remove the owner from his own business. This is called receivership, which dates back to the English Chancery courts where occasionally a judge would assign a receiver to protect and manage the assets of an insolvent entity. This makes sense if a gentleman of questionable ethics has unpaid debts and a valuable painting is his only asset. The court feels more secure having that painting under lock and key and not having its location and care unaccounted for by the debtor. Modern-day receivership in bank workouts is sought when a CEO is acting irresponsibly with the creditors' collateral. This can mean that the CEO is overpaying himself or family members, not collecting from friends, shipping on reckless credit terms, liquidating assets without bank consent, and so on.

The toughest receivership story I've heard was from a colleague who literally sat at the founding CEO's desk after he'd been removed from the business. The sheriff showed up on December 22 with an order to receive and secure the assets of the business. The owners and staff were made to exit the building while a locksmith changed the locks. A receiver, my colleague, was brought in to run the business. The CEO's family had been wrapping and storing family Christmas gifts in a spare office and were forced to leave them all behind – the court order clearly said "all property." The family celebrated the holidays without jobs, a business, or even gifts.

Receivership is incredibly difficult to attain by creditors in the United States and is principally governed by state law. I've been involved in a few situations in which the CEO was destructive, and receivership was appropriate, but in each case the bank's lawyers said that receivership was not regularly practiced in their jurisdiction and would be too hard to attain.

An interesting contrast is how Germany deals with insolvency. Germany has a much higher percentage of family-owned manufacturing businesses than the United States, and Germans take great national pride in their *Mittelstand*. But despite that, the German Insolvency Code was clearly written for the benefit of creditors. Although owners/operators have personal financial incentives to extend the life of the business, even if it's a slow glide toward liquidation, creditors have significant incentive to seize control of the business early and quickly sell it off as a going concern to a better operator. German creditors have the upper hand in these situations and can quickly force a change in ownership of a privately held business. If any of these three (low-threshold) criteria are met in a business, German creditors can force the business into an insolvency sale:

1. **Unable to make payments.** This means any cash crunch, even if seasonal.

2. **Forecasted inability to make payments.** I think that 90% of all U.S. companies have faced this situation at least once in their history.

3. **An upside-down balance sheet.**

The ideal is probably somewhere between the U.S. and German systems. The U.S. system is overly forgiving and tolerates the loss of jobs and community wealth, because employees and the community have no voice in insolvency. Reckless owners in the United States can destroy their business and they do it all the time for a myriad of reasons including ego, greed, stupidity, and laziness. Just because the lender and owner can take the hit doesn't mean the employees and community should have to. Too often, I'm dealing with "the county's largest employer" but the county and state have no say in proceedings. One drive through America's industrial rust belt and you know something is wrong with our system.

As I write this, we're currently bidding on an Italian auto parts business that is going through their bankruptcy procedure (in Italy, Extraordinary Administration). A very simplified explanation of how many European countries work is that they have accepted the social burden of the employees. This auto parts factory has 200 employees, but sales have declined so much that they only need 50 workers (2,000 hours per week) to produce the orders. So, 200 workers cycle through the factory in greatly reduced shifts, providing those 2,000 hours of weekly labor. The government picks up the tab for the other 6,000 hours of idle time through social payments. It keeps people "employed," takes immediate cash pressure off the business, maintains an assembled workforce, and holds the community together. We can bid for the business assets, but what's most important to the government is how many jobs we will guarantee for the next two years. It can seem more like an adoption than an acquisition.

Benefits of Bank Debt

Yes, things may be looking ugly in your business, but here's the good news: You now have a group of wise and experienced professionals committed to helping you save your business. Years ago, I was helping a friend whose business was imploding while he was in dangerous denial. His wife, business partners, and I tried many ways to get through to him, but none were successful. Watching the flames grow and frustrated by his staunch denial, I said, "You should have bank debt. A bank would be torturing you now to do the right thing, but instead you have private investor money with no covenants and no one is calling you to account."

Bank debt is also the cheapest form of institutional capital on earth, which allows them to have high standards. Think of banks as your toughest high school teacher or coach. They're a pain but if you play the game and play it well, you'll do better and be a better person for it. In fact, many workout bankers sincerely view themselves as rehabilitators, not collectors. You'll need to keep their support and do the basics like holding yourself to higher reporting standards than they require, being exceptionally honest when trouble is brewing, and controlling the story arch of your business. This is where credibility comes from.

A Quick Review of Secured Commercial Debt and Alternative Lenders

Types of Lenders

Banks

Think of your local savings-and-loan-type bank that holds your savings (deposits) and makes loans with those funds. Because they lend customers deposits, these banks are both your lowest cost of capital and the most conservative lender, they will offer everything from cash-flow term loans for healthy companies to well-collateralized asset-based revolvers. Their highest obligation is to the shareholders and depositors, not the borrower. The banks have an active commercial lending department, the bank president is a big shot in town and probably active in both the charity and country club circuits. The commercial lenders have low golf handicaps and an expense account. The conservative nature of these banks sets you against people who are highly motivated "not to screw it up." This is a team looking for base hits, steady progress and reliability.

Cynics will tell you that every commercial lender shares the same number-1 priority, namely, keeping its job. Priority number 2 is the bank's money and priority number 3 (on a good day) is you, the borrower. These lenders have to sit in credit committee weekly explaining what's wrong with (you) the borrower. Your actions determine how well your banker protects your interest. The credit committee wants to know if you are focused, hardworking, and reliable.

Finance Companies

Finance companies usually borrow money from a bank and then lend to businesses. They have an obvious higher cost of capital and therefore need to be looser on credit terms but tougher on collateral coverage. Finance companies are often the preferred lenders in distressed acquisitions because banks will usually want to see six to nine months of consecutive profits in a business before lending to them.

Hard Money Loans

Hard money loans are asset backed (secured) private loans, which generally pay between 10 and 15% over prime interest rate. Hard money loans are most common with real estate but can be gained on machinery and equipment.

Merchant Cash Advance Lenders

Merchant cash advance lenders are brilliant marketers but that's where my compliments end. A recent client ran out of money to fund his poor management, so he turned to a merchant cash advance lender, one who advertises aggressively on business radio channels. "It's really quite simple, we'll lend you $400,000 at 15% with no personal guarantee and loose payment terms. Just click on the link we sent you, read through the (many, confusing) pages of loan documents and provide your electronic signature." That's the promise they made but when I show up my client is paying 39.6% interest (39.6%!!) with a personal guarantee and they are threatening to foreclose. Somehow (innocently and naively) my client got rushed through the lengthy and confusing loan documents and signed the bottom. I printed and read them several times, the interest rate was hidden by a confusion of numbers and terms, and the personal guarantee was there, just not obvious.

The State of Vermont Attorney General's office was very excited to hear about these usurious and predatory lenders operating in their state, harming small business owners with their deceptive tactics. I was thrilled at the possibility of seeing these lenders held to account and giving my client time to deal with his bigger issues. After a very thorough legal review, there was nothing the State could do; the documents were all expertly written and technically not a loan but "the purchase of future cash flows." That's predatory behavior, for sure, but not in violation of lending laws or any laws.

Loan Sharks

Yes, they still exist and they still break thumbs and worse. You may remember an episode from the television show *The Sopranos* in which Tony Soprano lent money to a local business owner. With his cunning smile, Tony said, "I know things are tough for you now so I'm going to only charge you 1% interest – daily."

Evil, Mean, Sadistic Lenders

Honestly, I've never worked with an evil, mean, or sadistic lender. Every senior workout officer I have dealt with has been tough, smart, and demanding but also honest and honorable. Every one of them wanted to help me, and they all wanted to help the good entrepreneurs. Even the rotten entrepreneurs (earlier examples) were treated more respectfully and professionally than they deserved.

But there is an ancient sadistic streak in the institution of lending that is built around a sense of Old Testament–style justice in which the reckless are expected to suffer and repent. When a reckless borrower is slow to repent, the suffering should increase until there is a clarity of vision. Banks embrace this at their core, as do commercial lending laws. Lenders believe deeply that if you have been disrespectful with their money, then you should be suffering ulcers and sleepless nights.

The only authentic bamboozling I've ever seen from a bank was a large regional lender in the upper Midwest who flat-out lied to a CEO when they promised a 120-day forbearance period and then immediately sold off the defaulted debt to a predatory hedge fund who they'd been colluding with for months. Six days after the smiling Judas bank officer told my associate how pleased the bank was with his progress, he was being foreclosed on by some predatory hedge fund out of Manhattan. Turns out that this bank has done that before and is developing a reputation for unscrupulous behavior.

Federally insured banks rate and manage commercial credits in partnership with their government regulators. These files on creditor performance, stability, and direction are critical for banks to keep clean books and records for regulators but also for publicly traded banks to show the strength of their balance sheet by reporting performing and nonperforming loans.

The following sample bank commercial loan risk rating matrix (Figure 4.1) shows how banks view and rate credits. Each company's monthly financial numbers are plugged into the bank's big computers and measured against all their other loans. When the credit quality of your loan degrades, there are internal conversations about you and your business, which eventually leads you to a tough conversation with your bank.

RATING	GENERAL CHARACTERISTICS (It is not necessary for a credit to possess all characteristics to qualify for a particular rating.)
1–STRONG	• Well-established company with the following characteristics: ✓ Strong historical financial condition ✓ Company compares favorably to its industry ✓ Capable management team with sufficient depth ✓ Unqualified opinion from reputable CPA firm ✓ Industry condition favorable • Loans secured by cash collateral or properly margined diversified securities • Loans fully supported by CSVLI or an SBLC from a financial institution with a Moody's (or equivalent) rating of A or better

Figure 4.1 Loan grading system. Used by permission from Harrison Sangster.
Credit: Harrison Sangster.

RATING	GENERAL CHARACTERISTICS (It is not necessary for a credit to possess all characteristics to qualify for a particular rating.)
2–SATISFACTORY	• Established company with the following characteristics:
	✓ Financial statements demonstrate low to moderate leverage and adequate to strong debt service coverage
	✓ Company compares similar to favorable to its industry
	✓ Capable management team
	✓ Industry condition fair to favorable
	• Loans secured by properly margined nonmarketable securities
	• Loans to real estate entities with no material policy exceptions secured by properties with satisfactory historical cash flow, lease characteristics, and tenants
3–PASS/Watch	• Businesses with the following characteristics:
	✓ Limited or erratic financial history
	✓ Average or marginal performance characteristics to industry
	✓ Close monitoring of collateral necessary to ensure coverage
	✓ Industry condition fair
	• Loans to individuals with marginal to adequate repayment ability

Figure 4.1 Continued

RATING	GENERAL CHARACTERISTICS (It is not necessary for a credit to possess all characteristics to qualify for a particular rating.)
3–PASS/Watch	• Loans to real estate entities for construction, development or investment where repayment is reliant on proforma financial data or sale of collateral
	• Financial statements are stale, incomplete, or missing, making determination of current financial condition difficult.
4–SPECIAL MENTION	Assets which have potential weaknesses that may, if not checked or corrected, weaken the asset or inadvertently protect the institution's position at some future date. These assets pose elevated risk, but their weakness does not yet justify a substandard classification. Special mention is not a compromise between pass and substandard and should not be used to avoid exercising such judgment. This rating should generally not be used for more than 24 months as credits should move back to pass-rated or down to substandard.
	Businesses with the following characteristics:
	✓ Borrowers may be experiencing adverse operating trends (declining revenues or margins)
	✓ Borrowers who have an ill-proportioned balance sheet (i.e. increasing inventory without an increase in sales, high leverage, tight liquidity)
	✓ Adverse economic or market conditions
	✓ Nonfinancial reasons for rating a credit special mention include management problems, pending litigation, an ineffective loan agreement, other material structural weakness

Figure 4.1 Continued

RATING	GENERAL CHARACTERISTICS (It is not necessary for a credit to possess all characteristics to qualify for a particular rating.)
5–SUB-STANDARD	Assets have a high probability of payment default, or they have other well-defined weaknesses. They require more intensive supervision by bank management. Businesses with the following characteristics: ✓ Assets which are inadequately protected by the current sound worth and paying capacity of the obligor or of the collateral pledged ✓ Assets which have a well-defined weakness or weaknesses that jeopardize the liquidation of the debt ✓ They are characterized by the distinct possibility that the bank will sustain some loss if deficiencies are not corrected ✓ These assets are generally characterized by current or expected unprofitable operations, inadequate debt service coverage, inadequate liquidity, or marginal capitalization ✓ Repayment may depend on collateral or other credit risk mitigants ✓ The likelihood of full collection of interest and principal may be in doubt (these assets should be placed on nonaccrual)

Figure 4.1 Continued

RATING	GENERAL CHARACTERISTICS (It is not necessary for a credit to possess all characteristics to qualify for a particular rating.)
6–DOUBTFUL	Businesses with the following characteristics:
	✓ These loans have all the weaknesses of the substandard loans with the added characteristics that the weaknesses make collection or liquidation in full on the basis of currently existing facts, conditions, and values, highly questionable and improbable
	✓ High probability of total or substantial loss however, because specific pending events may strengthen the asset, its classification as loss is deferred
	✓ Borrowers are usually in default, lack adequate liquidity or capital, lack the resources necessary to remain an operating entity
	✓ Pending events can include mergers, acquisitions, liquidations, capital injections, the perfection of liens on additional collateral, the valuation of collateral and refinancing
7–LOSS	Business with the following characteristics:
	✓ Loans which are considered uncollectible and of such little value that their continuance as bankable assets is not warranted
	✓ The asset may have some salvage value but it is not practical to defer writing off this basically worthless asset even though partial recovery may be effected in the future
	The underlying Borrowers are often in bankruptcy, have formally suspended debt repayments, or have otherwise ceased normal business operations

Figure 4.1 Continued

Once your loan is rated special mention, the differences between large and small banks become more obvious. A large bank will usually move a credit to workout once rated special mention, whereas a smaller bank may send the loan officer to invite you to lunch, do a tour of your facilities, and try to understand what's happening. Once a credit is rated substandard, banks must take the loss on their books. They will rate the loan as nonaccrual (nonperforming), which means they have just taken their loss on your credit. Smaller banks may want to help rehabilitate your business, but larger banks will simply want to "exit" the credit. This means they are done with you and your business and you will likely be liquidated.

Your suffering business is now affecting the bank in ways bigger than most business owners can understand at the time. The following ratios are standard for lending institutions and reported to shareholders:

- Total nonaccrual loans to loans

- Criticized loans to loans

- Restructured and nonaccrual loans (dollar amount)

- ALLL coverage ratio (allowance for loan and lease losses)

As a loan moves from healthy to nonaccrual or as it is restructured or classified as a troubled debt restructure, then the bank wants to exit even faster as these loans impact their ratios even more and will require a detailed quarterly impairment analysis, which consumes valuable time and resources within the bank.

Smaller banks are more likely to work with you for many reasons. They want to be community lenders and will protect their relationship within the community. They also want depositors and shareholders seeing their efforts to support tough situations. Although a big bank may call for a quick liquidation so they can redeploy that capital, smaller banks are usually willing to be more patient. Even if we can get the business turned around, and even if we can bring in fresh capital, the company may still need 12 months of good performance to get the loan upgraded to performing. Part of this is driven by the numbers. A $5 million loan at a national bank is a mere rounding error and has no real impact on anyone inside the bank. I know this because I've gone to great lengths to get big banks to care about something beyond the loan balance, like jobs, community, tax base, economic vitality, and so on and they don't. They just need to process the paperwork and redeploy the capital. But at a small bank, $5 million may be meaningful. It may also make an appreciable difference to someone's year-end bonus, and you might survive just for that.

Being a big credit at a small bank has its own set of problems. Many small community banks do not have workout departments, and when a big loan goes south, they are wholly unprepared to deal with it. I've seen some act like reckless ninnies, worried about nothing but their own jobs, whereas others might be gentle and supportive to a fault, when more vigorous early intervention could make a difference. In trying to size your company to a bank, I recommend a ratio of $0.5–$2 million in borrower revenue for every $1 billion in bank assets. For instance, a $10 billion asset bank I know well is right sized for a business with revenues between $5–$20 million. Above and below gets out of its sweet spot. Equally, a $100 million revenue business will be oversized for a bank with $30 billion in assets. Many midsized banks will offer outsized loan facilities by syndicating or sharing the risk of a loan with other banks. Syndication gives smaller banks the ability to play in the bigger leagues, but that doesn't always give them the required skills.

In Detroit, there was a notoriously tough workout banker who tortured borrowers in the initial meeting. The business owner and spouse were both required to attend with their fully completed personal financial statement (PFS), and there would be no lawyers. The workout banker would take the statements and repeat a quick lecture about the felony risk of lying to a federally insured bank. Then he would ask for their wallets to see if their contents were listed on the PFS. Slowly, painfully he would try to determine if the $53 in your wallet was accurately reflected on the PFS. This was pure psychological warfare. He would review the clothes and jewelry they wore and make sure they were properly accounted for on the PFS. They would discuss hobbies: boats, skis, guns, tennis rackets, and so on. This could take hours; he might bring in recording devices or note takers just to up the stress factor. It would be hot in the room and he would not offer you water.

Then he would move on to the purpose of the meeting – to talk about your debts. He would recite in the same agonizingly methodical way how you signed each and every loan document, "Can you confirm that this is your signature again on page 24?" Then a page-by-page review of the legal documents with specific attention to covenants and legal remedies in default. This will likely be your first time ever reading that section and he would take the debtors through yet another extended and torturous review of their rights under default. Then he would review the personal guarantees, the guarantees that absolutely seal your fate. Then he would talk about the good faith of the bank, the great community works, the history reaching back 150 years, the strength and credibility of its bond, and the fiduciary commitment to depositors and shareholders. And, in a boiling crescendo, he would pound his fist on the table screaming that the bank would eat their souls if they didn't get their act together immediately. It was very effective.

Now the Ball Is in Your Court

We have one week until that first bank meeting and at this moment, the ball is in your court. You can take control and escape back to safety or you can get run over like a flat squirrel. Sixty percent of entrepreneurs in the week leading up to their first bank meeting choose inaction. They are discombobulated the way I was for 24 hours and have no idea what has hit them. Even when thinking clearly, most entrepreneurs don't know who to call or what to do. Most of these entrepreneurs are locked in dangerous denial, and a few are having actual crazy thoughts. But those with clarity will find help. If an entrepreneur calls me at that point, we'll quickly turn the tables, take back control of the situation, and get the business fixed ourselves.

There is only one way to understand your situation, once you have been introduced to a workout officer, you are the cow who has just met the butcher. Running away as fast as you possibly can (in the right direction!) is your best and only move. Your adversaries (the bank, commercial law, the courts, reality) are mighty, powerful, and omnipresent but they are also slow. You're the entrepreneur, you're agile as a cat, and you know how to get stuff done. But your brains are scrambled with stress, and you have no idea what to do next.

At this point you engage me, a corporate turnaround expert. In working together, what we'll do next week is walk into the bank with our heads held high and the following checklist of accomplishments (see later list). We'll have additional actions already taking place while the bank is kicking us around. We will smile because we have control of the business and by the time they've figured out what we've done, we'll be three further moves ahead. Some virgin will be sacrificed to the Gods of Credit but it will not be us, because we're running back into the jungle.

For the week-1 meeting, we will bring the following documents in paper form with copies for everyone in attendance.

- Most current month's financial reports
- Year to date (YTD) financial reports
- Any current documents that the bank may not yet have seen that you were going to share (recent tax returns, CPA reports, etc.). Make sure there is nothing outstanding.

- 13-week cash-flow forecast
- Collateral status review sheet
- Current accounts payable and accounts receivable aging reports
- List of tax, regulatory, legal, or trust fund issues
- Inventory report
- Forced liquidation analysis
- Personal financial statements of all personal guarantors
- A status list of changes being made at the company
- An executive summary on the turnaround
- Your 30-day plan; book next meeting in 30 days

We will survive by being the best of the worst. Of all the businesses in workout, we will be the fastest moving, most transparent reporting, and most cheerful. We will do everything right and the bank will come to admire us and support us. We will be the fish who is released back into the sea.

Our status list of changes being made at the company will look like what's shown in Figure 4.2.

Bank Strategy

Here's our strategy: We want a 30-day verbal forbearance agreement from the bank, giving us 30 days free rein to fix the business and get the bank out of our hair. We'll show stability and momentum today promising that if they protect us for only 30 days more we will prepare and deliver to them a complete turnaround plan and a way out. That's what we're after, and if we lay it out in a compelling fashion, they will

Status List Provided to Bank in Actual Recent Turnaround		
#	**Action**	**Status**
1	Fire CEO, CFO, COO	Complete
2	Replace with global restructuring team	Complete
3	Cease all noncritical spending	Complete
4	Contact customers/seller note holders	Complete
5	Cease payments and begin negotiation of seller notes	Complete
6	Freeze all past-due payables	Complete
7	Model Proforma forecast	Complete
8	Chairman, CEO, or CRO to every facility	Complete
9	Cease IT projects and reduce IT spend	Complete
10	Replace overpriced attorneys	Complete
11	Replace overpriced IT Consultants	Complete
12	Move HQ, sublease corporate clubhouse	Complete
13	Establish supply chain credit programs with vendors	In Process
14	Stop losses in factory #8 within 30 days	In Process
15	Stop losses in factory #7 within 30 days	In Process
16	Gain customer financial support for factory #6	in Process
17	Chairman, CEO or CRO to every customer	In Process
18	Accelerate A/R Collections to 10 days	In Process
19	Headcount reductions	In Process
20	Wage and benefit reductions	In Process
21	Eliminate 4/6 of senior management positions	In Process
22	Double size of the sales force	In Process

Figure 4.2 Bank update, status list of changes.

support us. Unless we'll need additional cash during those 30 days, then all bets are off.

We'll walk in with remorse and contrition hoping to avoid the torture and verbal abuse. As a turnaround consultant I'll call the bank the day I'm engaged and tell them how completely dialed in you (the debtor) are and how committed I am to keeping you focused on salvation. There is a chance that you annoyed the lenders so bad that they just have to torture you a bit. I've had to sit through those sessions. Either way, we get through that and then take control of the meeting.

We lead with the collateral status review sheet. This recaps the status, value, and location of the collateral, mostly receivables, inventory, and equipment. This is strongest if it's submitted as an affidavit with your signature. Make it just one page, very brief. Receivables are collected by our staff within a process that nets X days of sales outstanding (DSO), Inventory is stored in X location, valued by this method and categorized in these groups and values. Equipment is maintained in good working order at X location, most recent appraisal (attached) was performed on X date.

This gesture of leading with collateral is your bow to the authority of the bank. Our message is this: Here, sir, are your belongings, which we use only by your grace. It's a small step for the borrower but speaks volumes in the credit committee.

Then we pivot to the list of changes. This tells them everything they need to know about your commitment and direction and it is also where we take control of the meeting. You are a CEO possessed with making things right, and they need only give you room to work. This gets you off the liquidation list.

Then we show them our cash-flow forecast. There are only four options here:

1. Company generates sufficient internal cash flows to fund operations and can recover with a good plan and great execution.

2. The company embraces significant change but that alone does not create enough internally generated cash to fund a substantial recovery.

3. The company will undergo radical surgery but needs an immediate cash injection to maintain going-concern value and to fund the conversion of bottled up orders into shipments and receivables. The cash-flow forecast must show that the business will turn cash positive by no later than week 10.

4. The company is not cash sustainable and has no ability to become cash sustainable even with radical surgery.

Option 1, we're good to go. We'll come back in a month and update the bank on our progress. The key here is to hit the gas and get out of trouble as fast as you can. Make sweeping changes, tighten up your culture, cut some costs, raise some prices. If you're aggressive, you can lock in five years of good financial health in the next 90 days and make this situation an incredibly positive experience. It's very likely the bank will put you "back on the line," which means you leave workout after a quick scare and go back to playing golf with your old banker buddy. This presentation is option 1: sufficient cash and a good plan to reverse course – the company stubbed its toe. This company would either never formally enter workout or be "returned to the line" of normal lending. It is rare.

Option 2 is a false option because it is not a solution to the problem. The workout banker needs to get this file resolved, and you need to move the business out of its current situation. If significant change wasn't enough, then radical surgery is required. This often means an amputation. We are saving lives, not limbs. We will shut down divisions, sell off locations, liquidate inventories, eliminate departments, and exit lines of business. The cash-flow forecast has to indicate survivability within 13 weeks, and we have to keep adjusting the plan until we have a model that is sustainable. Focus on the jobs you are saving, not the ones you are cutting. The only alternative to deeper cuts is a quick distressed sale to a gutsy buyer.

Option 3, we're committed to radical surgery, because it is the only survivable path forward. But for many reasons the business will go cash negative until the benefits are realized. The business is often out of cash or even overadvanced by the time I'm called in or it's headed there with a momentum that can't be stopped. Or the radical changes create an extraordinary cash need, such as severance expense, especially in unions or more progressive countries such as Europe and Canada. We have to convince the bank (credit committee) that this is a risk worth taking. Some big national banks will just pull the plug despite the rosy prognosis. Some will fund the turnaround, but this goes against the very mantra of collections: "Our first loss was our best loss."

What if we project four more weeks of positive cash flow before the business goes cash negative for five weeks? That's a tougher sale because we're going to be depleting their cash collateral for four weeks and then asking for a cash injection and further depleting their working capital for a few weeks after that. What's critical is where we show "the turn" in our forecast – that is, where we start building back cash in the business. The sooner it happens, the safer the bank feels; the longer it takes to happen, the more risk and exposure they are facing.

In Option 4, an expedited going-concern sale is the most graceful way to avoid complete loss. You still have leverage and can get out of this relatively unscathed if you play your cards right. Getting an overadvance from the bank when you're headed toward liquidation is unlikely. If you can convince them of the return on those extra funds, you may have a chance. If we have a letter of intent from a solid buyer, we have lots of options. I've funded operations from bank overadvances but also from the buyer in dire situations and even from customers who are heavily reliant on the products. Once we rented out a lumberyard to a prospective buyer. We couldn't afford payroll and were ready to shut down, but he was interested in the business and needed time for due diligence. So, we rented him the business operations, and he came in with his crew and ran the place for 30 days to see what foot traffic was like. This was like a low-cost, risk-free test drive. Simplistically, this is an operating lease.

For me, our upcoming bank meeting is 100% a sales call. I am making every possible effort to persuade them to support our way of thinking about the business. The banks know that I am leveraging my professional credibility to the hilt but that I'm also not putting my credibility at risk. I tell CEOs to remember a few key points when pitching the bank: first, every single bank employee is more worried about his or her job than your business, each reports to someone higher up, and no one believes your dreams in credit committee. As CEO, you're being compared to every other CEO in work-out, so if your documentation and plans are on point, your thoughts will be heard and often supported.

When heading over to the bank, the entrepreneur and I will role-play the toughest questions we can think of and practice our responses. Remember, all we're offering is contrition, stability, change, and transparency. I'll do most of the talking since we need to preserve and rebuild your credibility through action. Said another way, the bank is likely in "Gotcha" mode and just waiting for you to screw up.

Q: Where is our money?

A: The stack of reports we brought you today clearly answer questions on the health of the business, but no one is spending time looking backward. One hundred percent of our efforts are focused on rebuilding your position.

Q: How did you screw up the business so bad?

A: Mistakes were made and we're identifying the best solutions.

Q: He's unfit to run the business.

A: My client has great strengths and some offsetting weaknesses. Might I remind you that he's the only one in this room who has ever built a business and employed 100 people.

Q: We need you to pay everything today.

A: Let's review the business's ability to service the debts in the cash-flow forecast.

Q: We have rights, and we can foreclose immediately.

A: My client also has rights and if forced to, he can maintain those rights. (I try to never use the word bankruptcy in these meetings; it's too emotionally charged. Everyone on the other side of the table knows exactly what is being said.)

Q: We demand immediate dominion over all cash

A: We think you should have complete control of the cash through me (turnaround agent). We acknowledge your rights and will inform you weekly, in advance, of every scheduled payment in our cash-flow forecast.

So, we're prepped, we've got our best plan for the meeting and you know exactly where you stand with the bank. We're in the parking lot, about to walk inside the bank and I turn to you asking you to recall that scene in the movie *Animal House* where the new fraternity pledges are being hit with a wooden paddle. After each new violent smack of the paddle, the pledge, through gritted teeth yells, "Thank you sir, may I have another." This, I tell my client, is your "Thank you sir, may I have another" meeting. Remember that; it's your only role today.

Chapter 5

Turnaround Management

With a reprieve from the bank (however nominal it may feel), you now have to fix the underlying business. I call this patching the holes in the bottom of the boat. The analogy I paint for clients is that if this business were a boat we'd have a $100 million boat with $100 million worth of holes in the bottom of the boat. What we must do is find the biggest holes and make them smaller. "Think about it," I say, "You've got $100 million of other people's money passing through your hands every single year and you haven't figured out how to keep any of it." That's the whole problem. It's not revenue; it's you being at the bottom of the food chain. You have all the risk but you're the one who's not getting paid. Everyone else has been paid well for years except you.

To find our way out of this problem, what we fix first is the business model. If we're losing money, then our model is broken, simple as that. Do we have competitors who are profitable? What's better about them than us? Are they charging more, servicing better, have economies of scale, better customers, do they pay less, are they shrewder, what do they have that we don't? That's the difference. If we have five competitors and three are making money and two doing okay, then what's unique about them? How do they make money? We can also consider our past to see if the business had ever been profitable. When was that and what's different now? If a company has a historical profit that it can point to, then the odds of a turnaround are high. Even with sales sawed in half, there is probably a fundamental model that works and some muscle memory that can take us back there. If we can get our percentages of revenue to match for each cost category, then why can't we restructure the business like that? This is the land of 1,000 questions. Our only hope of saving this business is fixing the model. Sometimes it's easy and obvious; other times it is harder than a Rubik's Cube.

If the company has never been profitable, then the odds of turnaround success are very low. We have no historical demarcations; the company has always been adrift in the sea of losses never once finding safe harbor. Who knows where we should drive this ship from here? We'll model toward our successful competitors, but it's all on guesswork. Can we successfully get to a place the company has never been before and build cash in the process? It's very unlikely.

Most turnarounds involve businesses that are only about 30% broken and it's usually the entrepreneur's Achilles tendon. You'll get an engineer who forgot about sales, a salesman who didn't pay attention to accounting, or an administrator who forgot about service. Figuring out what's not working in the biggest ways is how we patch or shrink those holes in the bottom of our boat.

Each turnaround company is dysfunctional in its own special way, but they often follow a storyline. Here's a sampling of broken business models and solutions:

1. **Three trucking companies.** They lacked courage on pricing and invested their thin margins into geographic expansion while driving their fleet into the ground. Drivers were leaving to drive better equipment for competitors. Price increases and cutting the least profitable lanes provided the solution.

o **Four machining and fabricating companies.** All four were running on thin gross margins with a lean backlog, which led to periods of starvation when the order book ran dry. The solution was an investment in sales, quoting, and estimating – all with the goal to quote twice as much business with an additional 10 percentage points of gross profit margin. This was to net about the same topline revenue with a much healthier gross margin. We were aggressively raising prices and accepted a significantly lower hit rate; therefore, we needed to quote twice as much work to net the same monthly volume. Then we could quote more aggressively to fill in the lean months, giving us balanced and predictable profits. With steadier work and better margins, we were able to upgrade the team, which created a virtuous cycle of retained earnings.

o **Retailers and distributors with stale inventory and no cash to refresh.** This is easy: we shrink footprint (locations or square footage) and remerchandise, then have a big clearance sale and reinvest that cash into new and better merchandised inventory.

o **A few companies with a brilliant yet self-destructive entrepreneur owner.** Each company had exceptional engineering, superior products, and good service but no cash and a broken supply chain. The products were priced right, but the cash was fueling the entrepreneur's vanity. When the entrepreneurs are the problem, either they respond well to electric shock therapy from the lender or they lose control of the business. Often, these misfit entrepreneurs have their companies sold in a foreclosure sale, and the most talented, least flawed can find employment with the new owner. Sometimes it works really well; the former entrepreneur enjoys the ability to focus in on his strengths without the risk or headaches of being an entrepreneur.

- **In a chain of sports bars, the cash ($500,000/ year) was fueling the entrepreneur's gambling and pill habit.** I audited that business repeatedly, backward and forward, and just couldn't figure out where the money was going. My frustration was so palpable that the owner's wife whispered in my ear about her husband's vices. We had a big and uncomfortable intervention. Each of us drew our lines in the sand: he wasn't ready for rehab, she wasn't ready to leave him, and I was ready to go home and see my family, so I did.

- **A manufacturing business with a lot of demanding and high-maintenance distributors whose service and aggravation expenses were costing the company money and focus.** There were about a thousand of these distributors, so we rated every single one on contribution margin and aggravation. The bottom-ranked 25% were sent a pleasant letter retracting our agreement and wishing them well in future endeavors.

The bottom line is that a turnaround will be some formula of raising prices, cutting costs, streamlining operations, and fixing bad habits. Those are the internal management issues. Our job is to control them, and we will develop a thoughtful plan to improve them immediately and then permanently repair them over the next several months.

Gearing Up for the Battle

We've stabilized the crisis, but now the real work begins. We must deliver what we promised the bank. Again, take stock of your physical and mental health. How's your spouse handling it? How are *you* handling it?

Losses and bad habits have their own gravity and they naturally resist change, so we have to out-think and out-hustle our problems. This takes mental acuity, but most beleaguered entrepreneurs are not sleeping well. They are spending sleepless hours processing dread alone in the dark, next to their spouses but so alone. I lost months of sleep before learning some mental techniques to help me out. What the business needs is a mind change at the top. The owner needs to see everything through a new lens of understanding.

Few executives have ever thought of themselves as a chief profit officer but that's what the leader needs to be in a recovering company. Someone who wakes up every day to squeeze pennies out of the business, to provide greater stability, and all the societal rewards that come from a healthy business. As the most important part of a business, perhaps profits deserve their own executive?

Take an average industry. The top performers are making, say, 10% net operating profit, the middle performers (the C students) are making maybe 3% and the train wrecks are losing 5% annually. It's a 15-point spread, and you can probably cost-cut yourself half the way there. This is the slow grinding part of a turnaround. It's unglamorous and decidedly old-school, but it works. Here's how we get from train wreck to mediocre; Professional purchasing can take two to five percentage points off the cost of goods sold with very little effort. Better scheduling can reduce direct labor another two to five points, plus there's one to two points in your indirect labor, one point wasted in your sales effort, and one wasted in administration. Costs are like fingernails – they must be trimmed continually. We're going to grind the operating costs down one basis point at a time, which is why you must be running the numbers on your business constantly. As an outsider, I am trying to quickly build a holistic understanding of the business by its numbers.

Mindset

I once counseled a beleaguered CEO about his people skills and encouraged him to act differently as we worked through our turnaround. The CEO still ran the 600+ person company like a fiefdom; it was him and 600 underlings. Managers didn't feel supported or communicated to and often felt like the CEO undermined them. These folks wanted to be on a winning team but didn't feel that team spirit coming from the CEO. I had lots of examples and carried on through my list while speaking with him. At the end, he calmly replied; "They had better get used to it." After a pause, he continued; "My only goal in life right now is to save my business. I lose sleep over that, I don't lose sleep over how other people feel. I'll care about their feelings later, when we have a new bank."

This CEO's opinion flew in the face of inclusive, kumbaya style pop-management, but he was focused like a laser on saving his business and he did. He had a brilliant turnaround, saved most of the jobs, put lots of money back into the business, and five years later he lost the business, in part because of his poor management style.

Unions

The United Steel Workers union and I recently shared a prestigious Turnaround of the Year Award by teaming together to save an old Ohio steel fabricating mill. We shared an interest in saving the business, saving the jobs, and finding ways to make the business successful again. We have succeeded together and the union has been an exceptional partner over the past 18 months. I've shared similar success with other labor unions over the years and consider them vital partners in turnarounds.

But when a company flounders, the troubles often create the disruptive opening that union organizers look for. When profits and morale decline, this creates the opportunity for a union organizer to whisper sweet nothings in the ear of disgruntled workers. A regional trucking company I worked on endured two union-organizing campaigns at the beginning of our turnaround. The bank had threatened liquidation, we had zero cash, and now our facilities, in two strong union towns (Buffalo and Newark), were turning against us. Their complaints were legitimate but driven by the company's poverty, not the malicious intent of the owners. We were caught flat-footed and needed to respond, quickly. Phil, the owner, took the union support as a great personal insult and from his perspective it was. He was a man of the people, a trucker's trucker. Phil could out-hustle anyone on the docks or on the road, and he radiated a charisma that naturally drew people to him. But, over the years, Phil had grown comfortable being home for dinner and parenting his kids. His lifestyle had remained modest but that's not how the union organizers spun it. "Have you seen Phil? No, I bet he doesn't visit you guys anymore now that he's bought a new mansion, and have you heard about his yacht? Oh boy!" All lies, of course, but for a prideful guy in Buffalo who's driving a beater truck with over one and a half million miles on it, and hasn't seen Phil in several years, you start to wonder, "Where is the money going?" The organizer whispers. "Not into your wages, not into equipment. I'll tell you where it's going: Boats, RVs, vacations, and his second wife"... blah, blah, blah.

Our plan was twofold; we would call our union specialist to help us navigate within the rules of the National Labor Relations Act. When the union buries us in phony grievances, the specialist helps us process through the bureaucracy and keep a positive message within guidelines that can feel like an Orwellian form of censorship. When equipment is sabotaged, and the local unionized police force refuses to respond, we stick to the business and make things better. The other part of our plan was to put Phil on the road. Fortunately for Phil, he has the charisma that can turn the tide. A day on the docks in Buffalo changed everything. There was Phil with his natural swagger and charisma, melting hostility before our eyes. He joked, teased, scolded, assisted, and out-hustled everyone on the docks. We hit all three shifts, and our work was done. The union withdrew their organizing plans before being embarrassed by a vote.

One tremendously scrappy entrepreneur I worked with unionized his own shop. He was in the food business but brought in the local hospitality workers union. He negotiated the deal from a position of power and at the same time blocked more aggressive unions from trying to organize his shop in the future. In exchange, the local hospitality union got expanded payroll and power. This crafty entrepreneur now runs his shop on a 100% pull system; every night they schedule the next day's labor. They set up the production lines, know the exact staffing and throughput needed. Then they tally up the number of workers needed and call the union shop to place their order; "We're going to need 113 tomorrow, thanks." At 6:00 a.m. 113 union workers will be ready for their shift. Wages are fair and the union hall is collecting their share of that every week. The next day, the company might only need 104 workers, maybe 120 the day after. Not a dollar of labor goes to waste this way. Compare that to how other businesses manage their labor with plenty of sitting around time when work is light.

Canadian unions are stronger than those in the United States, but they've seen enough loss in two of their largest industries (auto and forest products) to understand that globalization is not going away, and we need to fight it with something more than defeat. For the most part I've found a sincere desire to save jobs and work together with North American unions. Together, we've taken on entrenched political interests and one particular bank chairman, and so far we have won. It helps that saving union jobs in the rust belt is one of the noblest causes one can support.

Certain European unions are more resistant to change and have been known to riot, vandalize, and boss-nap in order to make their point. French workers were burning cars in the streets when I first sat down to write these words, and they are doing the same now two years later for different reasons, as I edit this. When I was living there briefly last year, the blockades at the time were staged to defend the jobs-for-life (waiting for a pension) compact that transportation workers have long enjoyed. It's a wonderful country but an example of how different union negotiations can be around the world.

Boss-napping is a negotiating technique we've seen in Europe that combines kidnapping and the threat of physical violence with a hard-lined bargaining stance. One friend of mine watched out the conference room window as the factory gates were closed and then blocked with a large truck. He was trapped with screaming French union representatives who refused to let him out or have food, water, or use the bathroom. Finally, sometime after midnight, the union representatives were convinced by my friend's doctor to let him go lest they have a manslaughter on their hands. In the Basque region of Spain, another friend was so unwelcome at the following day's negotiations that the union representatives banged on his hotel door all night, keeping him awake then they barred him from leaving his hotel room the next morning. He was unable to attend the negotiating session because union reps kept him contained in his room until the following day. To be fair, similar tactics happen in the United States. A colleague of mine was once visited at home by two gentlemen with baseball bats in Rhode Island, and a few colleagues have had tires slashed.

Again, despite some rotten tactics by a few rogues, union workers have been some of my greatest turnaround partners, and I always suggest embracing them as part of your solution in a turnaround. We've saved thousands of jobs together, shared in some wonderful successes, and had a few good tussles along the way.

The Income Statement Turnaround

Our turnaround started with cash flow and changing the business from cash-losing to cash-generating. It can also mean moving the cash balance from negative to sustainably positive. Positive cash gives you the freedom from creditor pressure and the financial means to fix the business.

Although cash flow is the crisis stabilization part of the turnaround, the income statement is where the actual turnaround takes place. Somehow the CEO needs to get revenues exceeding costs, and do it consistently. It's mathematically simple, but there are only a few controls to work with:

1. Increase sales. If you're in retail, you can increase sales almost immediately. If you make engineered parts for large infrastructure projects or pharmaceuticals, it may take you years to actually book new orders and increase shipments.

2. Increase gross profit margins. Short term, this means price increases and cost cutting. Longer term, it takes the form of product design and courageous pricing.

3. Cut costs. This always works and you can (largely) control the pace and aggressiveness of cuts. Most turnarounds are cost-cutting exercises in which the business is simply made to fit within its gross profits.

A typical first call with a business owner starts with them telling us how they have a $100 million business, but when they send the financials, the current run rate on revenues is about $70 million. "Well, it was $100 million a few years ago and that's where we need to be" is the explanation we usually hear. The entrepreneur is slowing tapping his feet waiting for the business to recover to $100 million. In those situations, I usually see a $50 million business that makes a lot more sense; it is protected with high margins, real expertise and loyal customers. Although I want to quickly shrink to sustainable profits and a business with great core strength, the owner struggles to give up the big number that sounded so great but never really worked for them. "You went from $100 million to $70 million. What about $100 million (other than your dreams) sounds sustainable to you?"

I much prefer to shrink to profitability because it is certain. The business has pursued years of speculative growth fantasies, and your lender and stakeholders have lost their appetite for any more of that. They want stability, and your business desperately needs it, regardless of the top-line revenue figure.

With cash and stability, the turnaround continues on a script of doing more of the right things (cost cutting, price raising, new-product development, selling, accountability) and less of the wrong things (risk, speculation, waste, distraction). Keep your head down, hoard and reinvest your cash, and everything should turn out just fine.

When you can't solve the cash issue in a turnaround, then very few options remain. In fact, you have a fiduciary duty to stop the bleeding, even if that means firing everyone and closing the doors. That's why we need a cascading set of options where we can fail-forward into some sort of resolution. Even if it ends up in liquidation, maintaining control and extracting value for your creditors can be a dignified end.

The Salvation Process and My Worst Turnaround Result

Only once, as a turnaround professional and at the time of this writing, have I failed all the way through a turnaround to liquidation, and here's how it worked to the relative benefit of everyone involved:

Hank and Eddie were childhood friends who got into the salvage business at an early age. Things went well, and they made good money for many years. Then they expanded into processing. They had been merely brokering product over the years, making their spread (the vig) between buy and sell but never actually taking ownership or possession of the materials. They were merely brokering the spread or arbitrage between loads, and they didn't need much to support that – a small office, phones, no employees, and a part-time bookkeeper.

Next they wanted to expand their business by buying bulk product and consolidating full shipments by actually taking ownership and possession of the material. This allowed them the brokering fee plus processing and consolidation fees and later shredding fees, but it cost them the investment in a 40,000-square-foot facility, forklifts, trucks, employees, overhead, and a loss of focus. The business now had a much larger monthly overhead to cover, and the owners got pulled away from sales into (nonlucrative) operational and employee issues. To compensate, they built a (mediocre) sales team that contributed more to overhead than profits. Then commodity prices cycled downward, volume dropped, margins squeezed, and their shredding operation became unprofitable. This further distracted the owners from doing what they do best, brokering loads.

In our turnaround plan, we presented the bank with a cascade of increasingly less-desirable options; if growth and cost cutting don't work, we'll pivot to an expedited strategic sale; if that doesn't work we'll pivot to a private sale; and if that doesn't work we'll accept defeat and peacefully liquidate the business. This addresses the bank's number-one concern, downside risk. As I've explained, the bank workout officer isn't so worried about the mess he inherited but he can't allow it to get worse.

Here's the basic framework of our salvation process:

First control bank expectations, establish worst-case scenario and secure downside risk.

Plan A: Growth with cost controls and bank support.

Plan B: Expedited sale to strategic buyers.

Plan C: Expedited sale to any buyer who will find value in the business.

Plan D: The last possible step, a partnership liquidation with both bank and entrepreneur working together and a release from remaining personal guarantee by the owners. The bank will likely take a loss, but it is rare to ever get here in the turnaround process.

Picture a bunch of targets stacked on top of each other (Figure 5.1). Your aim is good, we just don't know if you have the trajectory to hit your top target, growing out of our troubles. But we have good aim, so even if we don't hit the top target, we should hit the one below it. The point is, we will hit one of the targets and we've removed the mystery about what's going to happen with this business.

Establish the Base – Forced Liquidation Value (FLV)

The secured creditors have had enough surprises and will not tolerate any more. They need to secure downside risks and provide a floor of certainty to the shareholders. Figure 5.2 shows how the bank is looking at the business. (Note: I will not present the Hostile column to the lenders; we'll discuss it and they understand it well enough.)

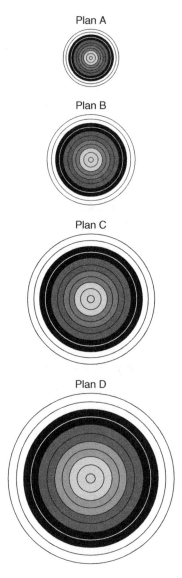

Figure 5.1 Stacking targets in the salvation process.
Credit: Logan Sands

Balance Sheet—Company #1			
Account	Book Value	Peaceful Liquidation Value	Hostile Liquidation Value
Cash	–		
Accounts Receivable	1,000	800	400
Inventory	2,500	625	–
Total Current Assets	3,500	1,425	400
Machinery and Equipment (net)	1,200	1,200	700
Computers and Software (net)	700	10	
Leasehold Improvements (net)	400	–	
Goodwill (net)	1,300	–	
Total Long-Term Assets	**3,600**	**1,210**	**700**
Total Assets	**7,100**	**2,635**	**1,100**
Bank Debt	2,000	2,000	2,000
Total Liabilities	**5,300**	**5,300**	**5,300**
Equity	**1,800**	**(2,665)**	**(4,200)**
Bank Recovery		100%	55%

Figure 5.2 Liquidation values.

The bank is owed $2 million, and if handled properly they can get a full recovery. If handled poorly they might take a $900,000 hit, or more. This is the entrepreneur's bargaining position and the art of playing poker with an awful hand. With a peaceful and orderly liquidation, we should be able to collect most receivables from the customers. With time, we can reel in aged receivables and greatly reduce the exposure and develop good will with the payables clerks. We can also convert WIP (work in process inventory) into shipments and recover prior investments in materials and labor. In a chaotic and abrupt liquidation, we lose those advantages. If the entrepreneur goes ballistic, he can poison the relationship with customers, destroy inventory, and damage or hide machinery, making recovery a much tougher prospect for the bank.

With coaching, the entrepreneur smiles and convinces the bank that he wants to do the right things and is not having crazy thoughts. This helps reassure the bank that their downside risk is secure and gives us a chance at fixing the business.

We stabilized the cash flow, dealt with all the trade partners and vendors, and got them comfortable. Then we went to the bank with the salvation process; we would pursue the best possible outcome with downside protection at the forced liquidation value (FLV or forced-liq). The entrepreneurs were willing to play ball and would protect the bank's interest in exchange for a shot at making the turnaround plan work.

With bank support we slashed costs to the bone while Hank and Eddie, the owners of the salvage business, went full speed on sales. No amount of cost cutting was going to make this business sustainable, so a quick improvement in sales was our best option, and it seemed possible. The owners got on the phones booking work and put our available cash to work turning loads. It worked but not enough. The resulting sales fell quite short of what we needed to reach sustainability.

That's normal; most entrepreneurs overestimate their ability to shift momentum and they underestimate the damage they have done to their business over the years of challenge. But, despite that, my job is to get them totally fired up and aiming for the best results. Hell, why not? If you're ever going to go big in your whole life, if you're ever willing to ever truly lay it all on the line, then this is that time.

So the owners doubled down on their sales efforts while I started writing the offering memorandum (OM, or often referred to as a CIM, confidential information memorandum) to present the business to strategic buyers. The OM is a 20- to 40-page document that sells the business; it's what an investment banker puts together and refers to as The Book. A fancy investment banker will take months to produce a 70-page book with knockout graphics, but in a distressed sale, the key is bringing quick focus to the core values in the business and not letting buyers get distracted with all the problems.

The whole book (OM) is written to present the highest possible going concern value. Remember, the company is in the zone of insolvency and our legal duty is to the highest possible recovery, not always the preferred buyer. Unfortunately, this might mean selling to a remote company who strips out operations and reduces the local workforce. It's my job to understand the possibilities and model them out for the prospective buyers. I'm an operator by nature, so I usually want to walk the plant floor with the buyer's top finance and operations executives to help them see every little opportunity available to them. We basically walk the entire P&L and Balance Sheet on foot, and I guide them to my optimistic understanding of this business. I'm selling revenue, gross margin dollars, contribution margin, the customer list, workforce, backlog, some unique capacity, redundancy savings, intellectual property, knowhow, taking out a competitor, and so on. Beyond that, it's just a pile of idle equipment in a semi-idle factory, in a world flooded with capacity.

The key here is going concern value. Less experienced buyers expect us to sweat when the walls are clearly crashing in on us. They poke around with questions like; "You're running out of cash, why would we pay anything for a business that will be closed in three weeks?" It's a rookie question because three weeks gives us plenty of time to auction off the company at a premium price and have a binding letter of intent. With a binding letter of intent, we can probably bridge finance the next gap and keep the business alive to a sale. If we move quickly on a sale, I can be talking directly with 5 to 10 qualified, strategic fit CEOs in one week. The company's insolvency, combined with our sale process creates pressure for them and brings forth serious buyers quickly. The pressure gives us options to craft the very best deal. It's a sellers' market for a going concern, even when the building is on fire.

So, by day 15 in the salvage company we've seen what the sales effort has accomplished. We can pivot there to a sale or if things look promising we can commit to another 15-day sales effort, with bank support. If the company is cash positive, and forecast to stay that way, we can breathe easy and think more strategically. But if the sales effort hasn't delivered the volume to get the company above breakeven, then it needs to find a new owner. We let the bank know that sales have not materialized in the first 15 days and that while the sales effort continues, we're moving to Plan B, a strategic sale of the business.

In between days 15 through 30, the owners are still pumping sales to increase our going concern value while I can write the OM, soft-pitch the business to 10 to 30 strategic buyers and have good feedback on the business and our prospects. We'll know who is likely to make an offer, their value and structure range, how it fits for them strategically, their general financial health along with the acquisition experience and bandwidth of the management team. I've had situations with no interested buyers at all (lumber yards in 2010) and others with plenty of interested buyers (aerospace machine shop with tier-1 customers).

The strategic buyer universe for our salvage company was small but we contacted every one of them along with a number of private equity (PE) groups with a penchant for investing in small distressed businesses. The PE groups didn't see a clear strategic play. Two strategic buyers showed interest, one seemed a bit overwhelmed. That party had never done an acquisition and they were not sophisticated businesspeople, just very successful blue-collar millionaire-next-door type guys. With a buyer like that I will often act as their advisor to show them how the acquisition and financing can be structured and get them comfortable with the concept. It's a great learning opportunity for them if they embrace it.

The other interested buyer was big, aggressive, and sophisticated. The CEO was a former maniac, brimming with kinetic energy who now poured his obsessiveness into work and marathons. He was the ideal buyer, 20X our volume and had no physical plant. He could fill our facility with work and save all those handling and processing fees on his much greater volume. Plus, he had a history of acquisitions, was super rich, and fearlessly aggressive. My entrepreneurs would get employment contracts, the bank would get a more complete recovery, and I'd leave with a success fee plus the invaluable thrill of saving another business. We went through weeks of due diligence until our big, aggressive buyer had sufficiently scoured our entire business, learned everything he could about us, and then walked away. Our chances of a strategic sale were dead, the bank was annoyed and we were about out of cash.

I'd been developing nonstrategic (financial) buyers through this process and hadn't found anyone yet.

A financial buyer can be a wealthy local individual or a private equity group. These private investors are usually entrepreneurs looking to own and operate a company. They are hard to find and usually not comfortable with or capable of going through an expedited sale process. To find them, I usually start by talking to banks, attorneys, and CPAs, asking for introductions to the wealthiest, most entrepreneurial people in town. It's pretty much them and their friends who will be our candidate pool for financial buyers. There were no interested financial buyers in the area, it was a tough, dirty business in a fancy New England resort area.

I had found no private equity firms who wanted this business as a strategic investment, and it was too small to be a platform investment for them. Platforms are usually the initial investment in an industry (which this would be) and they become the platform for additional add-on acquisitions. Even the lower-middle-market PE buyers are looking for healthy companies with revenues over $20 million and EBITDA (earnings before interest, tax, depreciation, and amortization) over $2 million to become their platforms; this salvage business was neither healthy nor near $20 million in revenues.

The last and final hopes for a distressed business are special-situation PE firms who look for small, distressed companies like this. These are known and funded buyers who can close on a transaction in weeks and even provide life support after a signed letter of intent (LOI). The conversation with them is very direct; the business is a stinker but here's how you can make it work. If I can map out and de-risk the acquisition, then I can usually get someone to take a shot. But this recycling business lacked a clear path to success. My last question is this: "Would I take this business today, as-is, for free?" If the answer to that is no, then it's game over.

That was it, we'd run through Plans B and C, selling to a strategic or financial buyer. It was liquidation time. The company owners, Hank, Eddie, and I had several meetings with our bankruptcy/restructuring attorney as he negotiated the liquidation plan and release with the bank. When I need to scare a creditor, I'll refer to our attorney as a bankruptcy lawyer; when we need the creditor to calm down, I'll refer to the same attorney as a restructuring attorney. They are one and the same because they specialize in insolvency issues both in and out of court and both in or out of the bankruptcy process.

We considered a last-buy program, which alerts customers to the factory's closing and allows them to make final purchases before the factory shuts down completely. This is standard in many platform industries like auto, aerospace, medical equipment, and for the creditors it's a great surge of profitable work with very little overhead attached. Employees get another 30 to 60 days of work, and the business can conform to the WARN Act (Worker Adjustment and Retraining Notification Act) regulations. But this was a recycling broker, so no one was interested in a final buy.

This was a failure, and the net result is that the bank took a loss, a little less than if they had just liquidated on day one. The owners lost their business, lost their jobs, were disgraced, and walked away with nothing after 10 years of hard work. Within a month, each of them had new jobs. One took a step down in pay, potential, and freedom from the entrepreneurial gig he'd grown accustomed to. The other owner embraced the idea of just being a pure trader, free of the hassles of owning and operating a business. Within a year he was earning half a million dollars in annual commissions with no personal guarantees or risk.

That's my worst-ever outcome as a turnaround professional. We really believed the business could be saved or sold, but instead one partner ended up in a worse situation and the bank came out maybe 10% worse off for taking a chance.

Cash Flow During the Salvation Process

Before we move on, let's talk about cash flow during the salvation process. If the company is producing cash, then the salvation process is not needed. Maybe debt restructuring is in order, but not some process that could lead to a liquidation. The salvation process is needed if the business isn't sustainable but still has a chance to save itself before running out of money. Although the entrepreneur and I may feel great about this one last big push to save the business, the bank may be too fatigued to even care anymore.

Or, if you need money to finance the salvation process, you're really out of luck. The bank has zero interest in going deeper into debt on this venture, and every lender will prioritize his or her job security above your last-ditch effort. But it can happen. With the right mix of circumstances and credibility, you can put together a last ditch plan that the bank will fund, totally ignoring the maxim about the first loss being the best loss.

Years ago, I got a call from a sensor company in New York. They were considering a bankruptcy filing and their investment banker called me to see if there might be a better solution. They had already run a full but unsuccessful sale process and were out of options. I looked at the business and hated what I saw; a poorly executed business plan, in the wrong direction, to the wrong industry, in a foreign country, with low margins. What I loved was the opportunity they were not pursuing. It was simple, recurring, predictable, niche, and had high margins. The company and entrepreneur were too far gone to fund a turnaround, but a strategic owner could do wonders with this company.

The FLV on the business was $2 million, although total debt was $10 million. Therefore, it was an $8 million loss for the bank. Our plan to the bank was to quickly find a last-ditch strategic buyer while we kept the business alive. We wouldn't need funding during the four weeks that I thought it would take to get a letter of intent (LOI) but we would be draining inventory and receivables to cash flow our losses during that time. Said another way, we would be reducing the bank's collateral position and possibly diminishing their recovery in a liquidation. The bank was betting their money to support our efforts. Meanwhile Tony, the owner, is still driving his flashy orange convertible around town and acting like a jerk.

My first likely buyer passed on the opportunity. He liked the company but didn't trust the owner. I only had one other possible buyer, a distributor of similar products with 10X more revenue along with facilities and operations to absorb the sensor company and get it out from under a nasty landlord. I delivered an offer of $5 million to the bank, which seemed like a no-brainer to me. The bank would recover 250% of the forced liquidation value and had probably already accrued for the $8 million in losses.

The bank refused the offer and then went silent. It wouldn't even take my calls and I've worked with them for years. The next day the bank's attorney began the foreclosure process. I know banks and entrepreneurs expect miracles from me, and I'd pretty much pulled it off with this sensor company. The bank would get a $3 million premium value while the company would survive, the entrepreneur would have a fresh start and earn equity going forward. The buyer would have a great little niche business that could be run like a cash machine.

But the bank was not happy, so the whole deal fell apart and everyone wandered off. At that point I'm playing the role of investment banker, so I begin shuttle diplomacy going back and forth between the three parties. The bank is coldly saying they prefer to see blood than take this deal. Tony knows it's curtains for him and his personal guarantee, so our only real bargaining chip is threatening (through his attorney) that Tony might destroy everything if the bank doesn't take this deal. He will sue and lash out and be dangerous in his actions ("you know, a guy like that can cause a lot of damage in a short amount of time"). This creates risk and uncertainty with the bank and they don't like that. Fortunately, Tony was enough of a jerk that the threat was believable. It's a stalemate. The buyer says to call if something develops. Me, I'm screaming at everyone about going concern value. The business is imploding, cash is draining, the customers are leaving, and jobs are disappearing. If they don't need me, then we should just call the auctioneer.

Three weeks passed, and the company continued to burn cash (the bank's cash) while deteriorating in value. The bank was burning cash on its attorney and this situation was top of the agenda in credit committee meetings. No one was happy. This was the suboptimal path, and I remained convinced that there was still a deal that could happen here. After much stomach acid on all sides, we finally structured a $7 million purchase price. It was still a good deal for Frank, our buyer. He got a great little business with proprietary products and a high potential sales leader in Tony. Tony got an employment contract plus stock options in the new entity. The bank got a 350% premium on auction value and the community kept most of the jobs while retaining a healthy, restructured manufacturing business. Me, I got a success fee, declared victory, and went home. We all benefited from the bank's patience and willingness to fund the company while we explored options.

> It ought to be remembered that there is nothing more difficult to take in hand, more perilous to conduct, or more uncertain in its success, than to take the lead in the introduction of a new order of things. Because the innovator has for enemies all those who have done well under the old conditions, and lukewarm defenders in those who may do well under the new. This coolness arises partly from the fear of the opponents, who have the laws on their side, and partly from the incredulity of men, who do not really believe in the new things until they have had a long experience of them.
>
> **Niccolò Machiavelli, *The Prince***

Chapter 6

Arsonists and Regulators

"**G**oogle 'IRS 941 Prison,'" I tell my clients, "to see what comes up." It's pages of explaining how employers can go to prison for not properly forwarding payroll trust funds on to the federal government. It's the dumbest crime in America, but stressed-out entrepreneurs do it every day because they are so desperate to maintain the status quo. The 941 is the payroll tax that an employer withholds from the employee's checks and is obligated to forward those funds to the IRS on behalf of their employees. The employer is merely a trustee of these funds and there is absolutely zero business purpose or claim to that money in any way. A good payroll agency will not even process your payroll without these funds, because the failure to pay them is so fraught with peril. Death remains the only way out of a 941-withholding problem, not bankruptcy, not a sale, not a liquidation, only death. If you stay out of prison, plan to survive on government-allowable standards of expense (See Figure 9.2, page 241) and on the government seizing future tax returns and placing a lien on your social security checks.

The most powerful collection agency in the world (the U.S. Treasury) has made it very clear that collecting 941s is a top priority. Every time I have any influence or even proximity to payroll I get written statements from the payroll company that they will not process a payroll without the 941 funding and will immediately issue a letter to the board chairman, bank, and corporate attorney notifying them of the company's failure to fund.

But desperate entrepreneurs still play with this money as though it were operating funds. They're following some fantasy about just using the money today and paying it back next week, but it's playing with a loaded gun. As I type this, I'm dealing with a couple who built a wonderful business over many years but lost control recently, ran tight on cash, and didn't pay the 941s. These add up quickly in a company with a decent-sized payroll, and now they owe $600,000 in 941s. But the owners are dead broke. There is no cash, everything is mortgaged to the hilt, and the IRS is starting to put pressure on them. The following redacted email from their Enrolled Agent sums up their situation:

From: ███████████

To: Jeff Sands

Subject: FW: Trust Fund Tax

Importance: High

Jeff,

I thought you would like to know that the ██████████ case is rapidly deteriorating; the information from the Company is inconsistent with officer statements and lacks credibility. There is also the mistaken expectation that the IRS will accept a $██████████ cash settlement in lieu of seizure of assets. Not going to happen.

I know [attorney] brought you into the case and you invited me in, so I wanted you to be aware of where things stand. If ██████████ can't accept that his company is over and offer up the assets and cash as payments toward the trust-fund liability (to reduce its personal liability), the IRS will simply seize the company, its fixed assets, and all cash, and then proceed against them individually for the trust-fund monies. The IRS has already taken inventory and determined it can recover in excess of $███████ from an auction.

Neither ███████, nor ███████ understands that the IRS has determined that [the company] cannot be operated profitably (a condition precedent to the IRS accepting a long-term payout/settlement for the payroll liabilities), and has therefore moved to seizure. They all seem to think the IRS liability can be negotiated away like an unsecured creditor. This is simply not the case.

The Revenue Officer was willing to entertain an Offer in Compromise, rather than seizure/auction, because I relayed to him what the company had told me: the company had only $███████ in cash and was prepared to shut down. However, when I received the financial data and bank statements, the company had over $███████ [5X] cash in the bank and said it wanted to stay in business, and keep $200,000.

I will keep you posted, but I suspect the end is near and I will be withdrawing soon. I have had no response to my emails of last week and today from ███████. I did have a brief conversation with their attorney yesterday, who said he would contact the owners. I have not heard back from him.

I did the best I could, and appreciated the referral. Perhaps the next case will produce better results.

Thanks,

███████

That's how it ends. After the long series of bills and letters, which were so bland and confusing, you didn't really read them. Then an agent contacts you, usually at home. You'll find out they've been poking around your business and other assets as well. Soon you're being requested to provide every financial report available. Consider this request a federal subpoena when you get it. You'll provide details (under oath) of every financial transaction for every account you have had any influence over in the past several years.

Then the IRS seeks to collect. Tax liens are placed on every asset you own. Remember, you documented every single asset under oath, under penalty of perjury. Lying on any federal form is a felony. Then you start liquidating your assets to satisfy the debt. Then the IRS looks at your income. Let's say you're a CEO of a $20 million business and pulling in $200,000 a year. The bank is okay with your pay, and they agree it's reasonable and market based. You live well but you've also got to put kids through college and your spouse has grown accustomed to a certain level of comfort. Meanwhile, the revenue officer collecting from you and her boss may have combined salaries that are less than your $200,000. But they are above the national standards that the IRS will use to benchmark your allowable standard of living. It's quite simple, they take your entire paycheck and give you back a small amount for food and living expenses. And they keep the rest. You're now raising a family of four on $55,000 a year. This causes you to default on your other personal debts. You file bankruptcy, and you still have the IRS demanding their money, collecting because you still owe the money and bankruptcy does not relieve you of 941 obligations. Think you can sneak some extra income on the side? If you don't disclose that income on your tax return, that's another felony.

I have worked with several IRS Revenue Officers while helping clients who made this insane 941 decision. My experience has been that the officers were always pleasant and professional but also very good at their jobs. And very serious. And like a bank workout officer, they want you to be humble, compliant, and focused on getting out of trouble. Unlike a bank workout officer, the IRS agent works for the US taxpayer, and they can feel a missionary zeal about their work.

It's not just CEOs who have this liability. If the company lacks funds to pay, anyone with financial control is targeted. This usually includes the CEO, CFO, controller, and maybe even the payroll clerk. Professionals like consultants, CPAs, or payroll services can be swept up in these issues if not careful. The IRS will size up everyone's ability to pay and then go for those who have the most money first. They only need to collect once. It's much easier to collect from one than many, and if the CFO has a large, perhaps inherited, lake house with lots of equity, that's a tempting target.

The key here is to avoid these collectors and other regulators of their ilk. Given the choice to abruptly shut a business down and cut every single job, or not pay the 941s, I would shut down the business that minute without hesitation. There is no business in the world so fantastic and valuable that I would take that risk for. None.

Not transmitting 401k deposits is similar, but you'll be dealing with the U.S. Department of Labor. It's called embezzlement and it's a federal felony. Google "401k withholdings prison" and you'll see why this is another terrible cash-management idea. The point here is absolute control and compliance with these trustee responsibilities.

Labor

All earned labor must be paid, and it is the highest priority in any commercial situation. Lenders and federal collectors all stand behind earned labor in the debt stack. In the United States it is sacrosanct, and even more so north, south, and east of us. As most employers know, the regulator's hammers start falling 72 hours after a lapse in timely payroll. Employee loans or liabilities cannot be deducted from final pay, and most states cover earned vacations and benefits in the obligation.

Employees have been protected with several well meaning laws, to protect workers against companies leaving town in the middle of the night, or shortchanging wages, or somehow draining all their assets, shutting down the business and stiffing workers on final wages. One such law created for these protections is the Worker Adjustment and Retraining Notification (WARN) Act which mandates that companies provide proper (60-day) notice to employees of a planned mass layoff. The federal threshold for compliance is a company with 100+ employees, though some states have their own version of WARN, usually with lower employment thresholds – around 50. Failure to comply with these regulations mandates fines equivalent to six months of payroll (triple fines on the

60-day notice). Improper actions by management may invite the Department of Labor to target the owners and officers personally for payment. Certainly, these laws keep companies from skipping town.

The risk of proper WARN notice compliance is that a company has to guess (a completely murky guess) when it might be out of business and make public notice of that date. Immediately, the supply chain stalls, employees are freaked out, and customers start to abandon you with great haste. It is the stink of death upon a company that perhaps doubles or triples its odds of demise, but the notice does give workers 60-day notice to work on a new job or career.

States have developed their own unique laws with the same good intentions, but often, they have been applied poorly and have set legal precedent. I know of a failed paper company in Massachusetts that had a near-death experience in 2008/2009, recovered, and then stalled again several years later. Although it was an old factory in a modern economy, management was doing everything they could to keep it alive. But, as the business failed, they filed proper WARN notices and were nearing the end of their options. Then a gutsy investor showed interest, and the dance of investment heated up. It looked like salvation was just around the corner and the business lurched along on anemic cashflow. Then the salvation investor got cold feet at the eleventh hour and pulled out. It was game over. All jobs were immediately lost and wages paid. What wasn't paid immediately was accrued vacation, sick, and benefit time. The company lacked the cash but went and collected receivables, and within two weeks they had enough to pay all those obligations and be 100% satisfied on labor.

The employees ended up whole, but there was that two-week gap on the benefit payments. A shark lawyer found them and sued under Massachusetts law under which the corporate officers are personally liable for triple-damages on the delayed payments. The original amount was $500,000 and now the former employee-CFO is being sued personally for $1.5 million in total damages. This is just a guy who was trying his best and had his final pay delayed as well. The judge agrees this was not the intent of the law, but it has been poorly prescribed over time and precedence has been set. This sets up situation in which officers and directors are incentivized to wipe out jobs and businesses faster, just to limit their personal liabilities. I am told that Connecticut has a similar law and other states may as well.

Other Ways to Get in Trouble

States mandate that employers carry workers' compensation insurance. In exchange for this costly mandate, employers are shielded from claims for injuries an employee might suffer on the job. As you might expect, the risks for not complying are massive, but insolvent managers often choose not to pay these bills (again, I would shut my own company immediately before not carrying worker's comp insurance). Penalties for failing to provide this coverage to your workers can include criminal prosecution, civil suits, and personal liability for treatment of the injury.

A quick side note on workers' comp and safety, most entrepreneurs I meet are not actively managing this cost and striving to provide a safer work environment for their employees. I know of a wood-working factory where losing a finger was accepted as inevitable for tenured employees. Safety has great leverage in the workforce. It can lower insurance rates, lower absences, lower attrition, and protect your neighbors or it can do the opposite in every way.

Environmental and labor problems are two corporate issues that can follow you home. We saw this in the BP Gulf of Mexico spill where employees were criminally prosecuted for lying in the aftermath. A coal-mine owner was recently sent to jail for environmental fines because he directed dumping to happen. A contractor I worked alongside in a decommissioning is now in prison because he improperly and inadvertently moved some chemical laden pipe. Instead of reversing his actions and dealing with the regulators, he tried to cover it.

It's a field of landmines, and businesses have to be exceptionally diligent in their environmental, safety, and labor compliance.

Working with Regulators

Years ago, our family business was selected for an IRS audit. The business was growing fast and the idea of an audit sounded like a big waste of time to my dad, a busy entrepreneur. Ever the salesperson, he cleared out a private office for the auditor with its own phone and printer. Fresh doughnuts and coffee were brought in every morning that week and the flirty secretary checked in on him frequently. The auditor was made to feel like an honored guest. At the end of the week, the auditor said everything checked out, the accounting was very tight, and that he would mark his file appropriately so future audits would be less likely.

The best news about federal and state regulations is that they are applied equally to the marketplace. If you run a clean shop, the regulators will spend more time with your competitors.

Like Lenny in John Steinbeck's *Of Mice and Men*, sometimes these agencies just don't realize their own strength and can destroy businesses, almost like Godzilla's swaying tail. I recently worked with a family business that was marked with a failed state inspection report for a similarly named business. It was not their business that failed the inspection but a similarly named business in the same town. It was 100% a simple bureaucratic misfiling, but the failed audit report got attached to my client and not to the other business. The state agency took 11 months to rectify this error, during which the largest and most profitable customer (35% of revenue) pulled their business based on the misfiled inspection report. The company went into an immediate death spiral.

The story that gave birth to this entire chapter on unregulated regulators happened at Chemco, an industrial chemical processing company in a run-down rustbelt city that had been losing its manufacturing base and population over the prior 40 years. At 165 employees, the company would have been a small manufacturer 20 year ago but was now quite sizeable in a city littered with abandoned buildings.

The company had operated for about 72 years but had been in tumult recently, having cycled through four owners in the previous three years. Throughout its history, the company had a friendly and supportive relationship with the local county environmental regulators. Chemco operated under a waste water discharge permit that required certain testing, reporting, and compliance. For decades this was never an issue. Things weren't perfect but there was a productive working relationship between the company and the county regulators.

By August our turnaround had finally taken hold after four grueling months. One month after the acquisition, scrap rates soared to 60% before the entire process line had to be shut down, taken apart, and rebuilt. This shutdown and the preceding high scrap levels had pushed customers to the limit of patience with Chemco and new management. We were backing up major auto manufacturers and we knew the customers were making calls in the market to re-source us. We were in a race against the clock to catch up on late shipments, rebuild customer confidence as much as we could, and show the stability they needed to see. Things were going well by late September as we were finishing out our second profitable month, and everyone could feel the sun starting to shine again.

Then the Environmental Protection Agency (EPA) staged a 2:00 a.m. raid, just as they do on TV shows, with a fleet of SUVs, all carrying guns and wearing their "Federal Agent" raid jackets. They shut down the whole factory (we were a 24/7 operation), had employees assemble in the lunch room while supervisors and managers were pulled into separate offices to be interviewed. Every computer was "mirrored" by a special forensics team flown in from Atlanta. Toward dawn, more managers were called at home and asked to come in to be interviewed. After about 10 hours of shutdown the EPA agents left, but on the way out they called the Occupational Safety and Health Administration (OSHA) to rush over and give us a friendly surprise audit. You know, one last kick while you're down. OSHA came in and found nothing, which was the only satisfying moment of that crazy week.

Everyone was completely rattled because we had no idea about what was going on. If we didn't know what had happened, we didn't know how to fix it, and we were afraid to even turn the equipment back on. We opted to perform our weekly maintenance then and keep the equipment down for another 24 hours as we tried to figure out what happened. This disrupted seven weeks of dependable shipments to our customers. Worse yet, we had no idea what to tell them.

We had already "no-showed" at the morning production calls with our customers, so they knew something was up. It was really hard to put a comforting spin on a conversation that went like this:

> Chemco: We lost 10 hours of production due to ... a visit from the EPA this morning.
> Customer: A planned visit? What happened?
> Chemco: We don't know – but I'm sure it's nothing.

Customer: Are they coming back?

Chemco: We don't know – Hey, we've done a pretty good job of catching up on orders lately, eh?

Customer: Are you running now?

Chemco: No, we're doing our weekly maintenance, but we'll be up and running in another 24 hours. We'll run through Sunday to catch up.

Customer: So, no one knows why the EPA raided your facility today? And you've just taken us to yellow-light status with two auto factories?

Chemco: No, well, but …

The next day we were back up and running and ran the facility hard to catch up on business. Ninety days later, the three largest customers all pulled their business in quick succession. That was 82% of revenue and forced the business into immediate liquidation with the loss of 165 jobs in a town that could not afford it.

So what happened? There were, in fact, dirty waters being released into the county treatment system (never into a natural waterway) and the county tracked it back to the factory. Instead of calling management, they set up monitoring and tracked the factory's releases for over a month. With regularity, exceedingly high discharges were being released late at night. Some as high as 3,000 times the legal limit. Instead of calling management (as had been protocol for the company's 72-year history) the county called the state who called the EPA and, collectively, they all dreamed of a big headline-grabbing bust. Then the dirty discharges suddenly stopped. For days,

I can only imagine, they waited patiently, stretched thin by the suspense of what might be happening inside the factory. After a week they couldn't take it anymore and came charging through every door in the building at 2:00 a.m.

No one knew it then, but our third-shift wastewater treatment supervisor had recently checked himself into rehab for a heroin relapse, on the same day that the dirty releases suddenly stopped. No one knows what actually happened, but the best we can figure is that he was concocting strings of hoses to bypass the entire wastewater treatment and monitoring system and would knowingly, willfully discharge bad liquids into the county system. Why? No reason; the best I can figure is something similar to arson that satisfied some insane urge with zero upside value. That's it, an employee had done an awful thing and then left. The EPA was empty handed and upset. I kept telling them to imprison the perpetrator, but to them, busting some junkie drying out in rehab wasn't very appealing. But after making such a public spectacle with our raid, they needed to close the file with an indictment, so eventually they got around to prosecuting the remaining legal shell that once supported 165 families.

I've rehashed this thing repeatedly and come up with the following:

1. In retrospect new management should have taken a box of donuts over to the county regulators the first month and invited them over for a factory tour, new management presentation, and a lunch. If we had done that, they would have been much more likely to pick up the phone and not played their dangerous game of Gotcha. I now meet with environmental regulators as standard protocol when I take over industrial facilities.

2. Could we have caught this employee's 45-day bender through more frequent drug screenings and better supervision of supervisors? Maybe, though he faked the log books and had the discharge-monitoring sensors sitting in buckets of clear water while he simply bypassed them with dirty hoses. It was an unsuspected and brilliantly concealed crime of insanity that led to the most destructive blunder I've ever witnessed.

Every day there are random, unknowable liabilities circling the cosmos looking to wipe out a business. As a CEO or owner, you must be ever-vigilant.

Chapter 7

Insolvency and the Law

In 2010 I was liquidating a lumberyard for the bank and owners; it's not unusual for a beleaguered entrepreneur and bank to agree to a voluntary liquidation in exchange for something like releasing the entrepreneur from a personal guarantee. We were selling off inventory and had already contracted an auctioneer to sell off whatever remained after 30 days. I got a call from a local business owner who had recently sold a bunch of product to the store but was never paid. My heart went out to the guy; he'd gotten screwed. I explained the situation, that the secured lender (bank) had liened every asset and was still likely to come up short, so there would be no recovery for him. He said, "I was just in your store, I've seen my product on your shelf, let me just take it back and sell it to someone else." Gosh, it made so much sense and I really felt for the guy, but the inventory, his product, now belonged to the bank. They had the liens on it.

"No, it belongs to me! I was never paid for it," he declared.

"Well, actually not. It belongs to the bank," I responded.

You can imagine his response.

I explained: "They ordered, you delivered, and you delivered on credit terms. You transferred the ownership to them when they obligated themselves for it and they gave you a receivable in exchange. In doing that you completed the transaction and subordinated your interests to that of the bank. I know, this is the downside of vendor financing, and it is terrible. If it makes you feel better, have your attorney call me and I'll explain our situation to him."

He didn't like it and neither did, I but that's how the law is written and you're not going to change it.

The United States deals with distressed commerce through two sets of laws. There is the U.S. Bankruptcy Code that is federally administered through U.S. Bankruptcy Court. There is also the Uniform Commercial Code (UCC) that states interpret in their courts. Until a business enters the federal bankruptcy system, they operate under the Uniform Commercial Code and other state laws.

So what is distress and how do you know if you're in it? The technical term is the *zone of insolvency,* which is a strange gray area that often defies conventional wisdom. Normally management has a fiduciary duty to the shareholders, and that's how they conduct themselves. But in an insolvency that duty expands to include creditors, in addition to shareholders and the corporation. Said another way, the shareholders have failed to adequately protect the creditors, and now they must act also in the best interest of the creditors. There are few clear markers on the path to insolvency, but it can be argued that one day you were running the business normally and the next day rights and duties shift. Perhaps, it's because your biggest customer didn't pay you and you're cash-broke. But the next day you collect a bunch of cash and you're no longer insolvent, sort of. You can see the murkiness here.

Insolvency is defined as either cash-flow insolvency, when you can't, or don't, foresee the ability to pay your bills on time. Any entrepreneur knows that most small businesses move in and out of that ability over the course of a month. And how would you define it? A conservative cash-flow forecast might show a path toward insolvency while hopeful projections wouldn't. This could simply be the difference between how a CPA and an entrepreneur interpret the same set of facts.

Balance sheet insolvency is the other type of insolvency, when your liabilities exceed your assets. It is argued whether this is all balances or just current balances. Or, whether we use liquidation values or book values. Should we even consider goodwill or leasehold improvements, which have no liquidation value but often keep a balance sheet positive? Interestingly, most startups would be defined as balance sheet insolvent, which again illustrates how fuzzy the definition of insolvency can be.

As discussed in Chapter 1, the hierarchy of creditors is one of the best-named laws ever: the Absolute Priority of Debt Rule, which is codified in federal bankruptcy statutes. Most collectors don't understand this (and even many commercial and collection attorneys act like they don't fully understand it) so I get to remind people that the rule is named such because it is both Absolute and Priority and they really should quietly wait in line while we try to fix the business.

Liquidation value versus going concern value is another way of valuing a company and shows the stark reality of value erosion that (almost certainly) entrepreneurs and (likely) banks have ignored. The following values represent a healthy economy with healthy equipment values.

Figure 7.1 shows the destruction of value as a business slips into insolvency.

ACME Mfg. – Loss of Value in Insolvency		
Account	**Book Value**	**Liquidation Value**
Cash	–	–
Accounts Receivable	1,000	800
Inventory	2,500	625
Total Current Assets	**3,500**	**1,425**
Machinery and Equipment (net)	1,800	1,200
Intellectual Property	500	20
Furniture and Fixtures	200	–
Computers and Software (net)	700	10
Leasehold Improvements (net)	800	–
Goodwill (net)	1,300	–
Total Long-Term Assets	**5,300**	**1,230**
Total Assets	**8,800**	**2,655**
Liabilities in Priority Rank		
First Bank Revolver	2,100	2,100
First Bank Term Note, SBA-backed	1,500	1,500
Second Bank – Cash Advance Loan	250	250
State BDC Loan, no PG	100	100
Family Loan	1,000	1,000
Accounts Payable	1,500	1,500
Total Liabilities	**6,450**	**6,450**
Equity	**2,350**	**(3,795)**

Figure 7.1 Liquidation value.

Entrepreneur balance sheets are often overstated for a variety of reasons; bad accounting and ownership fantasy are the main causes. Over time, errors on the asset side of the ledger stack up, usually with a CEO who doesn't quite understand the underlying accounting issue but is happy to see equity increasing. The bank underwriters understand all the accounting issues and are only partially deluded over time. It's not uncommon for a lending officer (sales department) to look at the balance sheet (see Figure 7.1) during a review, nod his head approvingly about $1 million in equity, and move on, never really noticing how weak the balance sheet actually is. The dilution of value on a balance sheet as it nears insolvency is silent and unseen but it can add up to a considerable shortfall in a liquidation, primarily in the following ways:

- Receivables are automatically worth less in a liquidation because they become harder to collect when the customer–vendor relationship is ending. Collectors also need access to clean and current accounting records, which can be hard to come by in a liquidation. Also, customers use the liquidation as an excuse not to pay, and they don't like paying banks. Although the cost of collection goes up, results decline, and this reduces the recovery on this most-liquid asset.

- Inventory loses value quickly without customer demand. Finished goods may be sellable, or not, whereas WIP (work in progress) is probably worthless (who wants a half-built anything?) and raw-material inventory usually only has scrap or high-return-cost value.

- M&E (machinery and equipment) immediately loses value. The cost of a liquidation auction might be 25%

all in, and that's subtracted from the value received at auction. This can result in a steep decline from the book value listed on the balance sheet.

- Intellectual property is almost always overstated on a balance sheet. It might contain a few patents, of limited remaining shelf-life and of limited value, though there may be brands. It's common for entrepreneurs to rave about the value of their patents or brand names even though they have yet to extract profit dollar number one from them. Trademarks, copyrights, and so forth have little attributable value in a distressed business.

- Furniture and fixtures are worth nothing or close to nothing in a liquidation. I've knocked myself out trying to sell really nice office furniture and have probably never exceeded 10% of the original purchase price. The last liquidation I did we just abandoned the furniture and fixtures (F&F) to the landlord. One crazed CEO, spent $20,000 per office on furniture and another $500,000 on black walnut conference room paneling. All of which netted zero in liquidation.

- Computers, well you know how fast they lose value. A two-year-old PC work station might be worth $50 on Craigslist? The software license cannot be transferred, so it's hard to gain value from that investment.

- Leasehold improvements? Well that was your special gift to the landlord because you can't sell them or take them with you.

- Goodwill is hangover from a former acquisition that, apparently, has left little real value on the balance sheet.

What keeps an insolvent business above auction value is a pulse, any form of ongoing life or activity in the business. This is called going concern value and is covered in Chapter 9.

Corporate distress is a fact of life and economies have found productive ways of dealing with these issues over the years. The U.S. Bankruptcy Code is considered the best around and what other nations seek to replicate in their own countries. In Article 1 of the U.S. Constitution, our founding fathers called for bankruptcy laws to be written. America had broken free of Britain and memories of the horrible debtor's prisons in England inspired a feeling that society is best served when honest but unfortunate people and businesses are provided a fair and final release. Before we get too deep in the weeds on the rules of modern day bankruptcy, let's review the concept of insolvency and how it's been handled through millennia.

History of Bankruptcy

Leviticus 25:10 in the Old Testament, New American Standard translation, proclaims:

> You shall thus consecrate the fiftieth year and proclaim a release through the land to all its inhabitants. It shall be a jubilee for you, and each of you shall return to his own property, and each of you shall return to his family.

This verse is accepted to mean that every 50 years property will be released from debt, indentured servants released from obligation, and slaves released from captivity. Let me focus on my interpretation of the debt part here, and let's consider debt as it existed before the laws and limits we know today in the United States, when debt calculations were not uniform, interest not regulated, and so on. How would people be protected from predatory debt practices? How would people, families, and even tribes be protected from what could become generational indebtedness? The Lord's solution was simple, a jubilee in which all debt must be fully released every 50 years. This allowed debtors a "fresh start," and it modulated the greed of creditors who knew that eventually they would be back to zero. In one simple verse, it created balance. Today the U.S. legal system has achieved a similar (but uneasy) balance, though with far more detail and not nearly such a long wait.

My understanding of history is that Mosaic Law (Law of Moses) called for a sabbatical year that provided the release of all debts owed by members of the Jewish community, not gentiles, every seventh year. (Remember, Moses predated political correctness, so this sort of discrimination did happen.)

In ancient Greece a man and his family could be forced into debt slavery until the debtor repaid his debts through physical labor. The modern-day version of this might be working in the kitchen when you can't pay for your meal. Back in ancient Greece city-states enforced variants on this theme with limits usually around five years and protection of life and limb for debt slaves, a benefit not enjoyed by physical labor slaves.

The term *bankruptcy* comes from the Italian *banca rotta*, which means "broken bank" though many translate it as "broken bench." The common story I hear in the insolvency community is that in ancient Rome when a merchant did not pay his debts (and we assume failed to provide a specific plan to satisfy his creditors) his merchant bench would be broken, putting him out of business in the market and making a public statement for other merchants.

As you might imagine, Genghis Khan dealt with bankruptcy more seriously. His Yassa (book of laws) mandated the death penalty for anyone experiencing insolvency three times.

England formally dealt with insolvency in the Statute of Bankrupts published in 1542. In grade school, I learned about debtor's prisons in England in which debtors would be forced into a cruel and ironic purgatory of sitting in prison until they repaid their debts – with, of course, no way to earn money to repay those debts. Modern-day China, I am told by an American who recently fled a bankruptcy there, will "detain" registered agents of insolvent companies, giving them the inside of a locked room and a phone to fundraise for the amount owed. This could amount to years of dialing for dollars and hoping for release.

Conventional wisdom is that the U.S. founding fathers, after earning their independence from Britain, were determined to do things right in America. Although they had a long list of grievances with Britain, bankruptcy must have ranked pretty high since it was called for in Article 1 of the U.S. Constitution. *Article I, Section 8, Clause 4;* "The Congress shall have the Power to ... establish ... uniform laws on the subject of Bankruptcies throughout the United States ..."

Bankruptcy laws were established as America's nascent economy grew, and these laws continue to be updated over time. The first U.S. bankruptcy laws were established in 1800, the second laws in 1841 in response to the financial panics of 1837 and 1839. The third bankruptcy laws were established in 1867 in response to the panic of 1857 and the Civil War.

Perhaps the most fascinating development in U.S. bankruptcy law came during the age of railroads. Bondholders supplied much of the debt needed to finance these massive projects and collateralized their debt with sections of rail. When railroads failed to make bond payments, the bondholders were entitled to foreclose on and liquidate those sections of rail. Imagine a railway from New York to Pittsburgh and some bondholder wants to rip up and sell off (for scrap value) 20 miles of track near Altoona. This action would destroy value to the entire line, to all debt and equity holders, as well as to the larger economy.

Isaac Redfield in his 1859 Treatise on the Law of Railways explained: "The railway, like a complicated machine, consists of a great number of parts, the combined action of which is necessary to produce revenue." Courts, understanding that combined action along with the impacts of contagion damage and the semi-public nature of railroads, applied principles of reorganization to deal with these insolvencies. The Bankruptcy Act of 1898 and its amendment in 1933 allowed for the reorganization of railroads, corporations, and individual debtor agreements. This provided what is the most significant part of bankruptcy law in my line of work – reorganizing broken companies.

Although U.S. bankruptcy law is well established and emulated, some nations are just now coming to grips with the concept. The United Arab Emirates just created a bankruptcy law in 2016 and Saudi Arabia has announced it will introduce a bankruptcy law in 2018. "The measure not only aimed to remove the threat of jail for executives of business in distress but also to increase the foreign financial inflows in the country." Yes, the threat of jail remains how distress is handled in many developing nations. (*Startup MGZN*, September 24, 2017)

Modern-Day U.S. Bankruptcy Law

Avoid bankruptcy if at all possible. It is expensive, demanding, fraught with risk, and almost everything that can be accomplished in bankruptcy court can be accomplished out of court through persuasion. Although bankruptcy may save your skin as a last resort, it is often better used as a threat, direct or unspoken, than as a directed course of action. Expect a minimum cost of $100,000 for a Chapter 11 filing, though we're currently involved in the bankruptcy of a $70 million revenue company that has already spent over $9 million on legal fees.

Bankruptcy law is complicated and a little bit murky. A bankruptcy attorney friend of mine says that murkiness appealed to him as he was selecting a specialty of practice.

"Insolvency allows for a lot of interpretation and I thought that would allow me more creativity and challenge in my practice. Plus, insolvency is so counterintuitive that commercial attorneys simply don't understand it, and that gives me a huge leg up in insolvency issues outside of the bankruptcy court." Personally, I'm intrigued by any area of law that uses such intimidating terms as *absolute priority, cramdown,* and *strongarm powers.*

I am not an attorney, so I've found simple ways of understanding bankruptcy's modern-day structure and how it works. In short, there are two types: reorganization and liquidation. Reorganization (Chapter 11) is basically calling a time-out, reducing secured debt to the value of the collateral securing it, reducing or eliminating unsecured debts, dumping unprofitable leases or contracts, and coming out the other end with a clean balance sheet. Those remnants might be your business intact, just as planned, or it may be much less because you didn't have a good plan. But overarching all these machinations are the personal guarantees, such as the ones I signed in my youth, which will generally not be adjusted by a corporate restructuring. The guarantor will have to reckon with these in one manner or another after restructuring.

Liquidation (Chapter 7) is simply that; the auctioneer is called in, employees are terminated, properties abandoned. But opportunities may exist for stakeholders to acquire valuable assets at bargain prices from the trustee. The renowned outdoor equipment company Black Diamond was founded on assets purchased by its employees after product liability lawsuits forced the original business into bankruptcy (that was an 11, not a 7, but nevertheless a liquidation).

Reorganizations are handled differently among various groups, as a family farm with a failing crop should be treated with different nuance than when, say, the city of Detroit files for bankruptcy. Although these cases can vary dramatically, they mostly have one thing in common – a cadre of divergent stakeholders with vastly differing interests who must be corralled, cajoled, or litigated into cooperation by the plan proponent's counsel.

Exhibit 7.2 helps explain the general structure of bankruptcy chapters in the U.S. Code.

The missing chapters in Figure 7.2 are all part of Title 11 of the U.S. Bankruptcy Code. Chapters 2, 4, 6, 8, and 10 no longer exist because they were either repealed or consolidated into other chapters. Chapters 1, 3, and 5 provide for

Chapters in U.S. Bankruptcy	
7	Liquidation, any and all
9	Reorganization for municipalities
11	Reorganization for corporations
12	Reorganization for family farmers and fishermen
13	Reorganization for individuals
15	Reorganization of U.S. operations of foreign companies

Figure 7.2 U.S. bankruptcy chapters

definitions, administration, and a more thorough explanation of creditors, debtors, and the estate.

Chapter 11: Corporate Reorganization

We are surrounded by companies that have survived only through Chapter 11. These include massive energy companies, national retailers, railroads, airlines, municipalities, and, of course, the real estate empire of a certain politician. Chapter 11 is how Hostess got restructured and was able to regain health. Companies in the airline and retail industry often restructure under Chapter 11 repeatedly and are sarcastically referred to Chapter 22 or 33 filers. Consumers are apparently unconcerned about flying on an airline that is under bankruptcy protection. The legal construct of this process is why companies like Quicksilver, Aeropostale, Chrysler, General Motors, Delta, United, US Air, and Chuck E. Cheese are all still in business as I type this. Clinically, it is fair and increasingly efficient but also costly, risky, and uncertain.

Although Chapter 11 remains a useful tool of last resort, the number of filings and the industry as a whole has been on the decline in the last two decades. Part of this is because lenders have wised up and are drafting bankruptcy resistant loans and partly because of the astronomical expense of a complex restructuring. The filing company, or debtor, generally pays most of the bills on all sides. Your ripped open company is now funding your lawyers, your bank's lawyers, the creditor's committee's lawyers, US Trustee fees and so on. Plus, all parties are likely using a financial advisor and the business is often paying for all of that. And if the debtor is not paying it, the various creditors are. It can be an obscene feeding frenzy of professionals that further drains an already struggling company. In a contentious bankruptcy, you are funding the other side's accusations against your management, which become part of the public record, that you are paying for. It is not for the faint of heart.

Entrepreneurs who personalize the business and its situation have an awful time in Chapter 11. Every part of the process feels like a personal affront, and entrepreneurs spend more time fighting their attorneys and the process rather than taking this rare opportunity to get their houses in order. Rather than minding your business fundamentals, you are learning about cash collateral budgets, defending variations in expected cash flows, and learning about the arcane laws governing absolute priority and the like.

However, wherever there is adversity, there often lies opportunity. More experienced entrepreneurs see bankruptcy as the chance for a thorough cleaning and likely part of a larger strategic plan. Two very clever entrepreneurs I know grew their business on debt then restructured it away in Chapter 11 as growth stalled. They ended up with a healthy, leaned-down business, a clean balance sheet, and retained 100% control. Again, the lack of or limitation on personal guarantees affords one greater flexibility in such a strategy.

The craftiest capitalists see Chapter 11 as a tool to take over train wrecks and then perform radical surgery on the business, bringing it out lean and clean. These investors have

100% of their energy and emotion focused on the future state of the business – and no personal guarantees with which to contend. This keen ability to see opportunity in carnage and understand how to both fix the business and use the rules of the game to your advantage can net healthy returns.

Bankruptcy can be used as a weapon by both debtors and creditors. Creditors can ally and force the company into an involuntary bankruptcy. If caught flat-footed, the company can be ripped apart in liquidation, with recovery to the creditors but the loss of jobs and community vitality. In the role of chief restructuring officer to businesses I've been threatened with an involuntary bankruptcy several times, but it always seems to be from a half-informed unsecured creditor that knows just enough to cause damage. This is probably why it takes two to three undisputed, unsecured creditors to force an involuntary bankruptcy, the logic is that it's hard to find and coordinate that many self-destructive loons. And if the threat is carried out, the target of an involuntary bankruptcy can deftly convert the case to a Chapter 11 and quickly turn it to its advantage. In large complex capital structures, investors can seek to purchase the fulcrum securities and then force the company into bankruptcy, thereby gaining inexpensive equity control of the business post restructuring.

Debtors can use bankruptcy, or even the threat of bankruptcy, as a weapon to accomplish their goals. Let's face it, simply retaining a bankruptcy attorney is moving onto offense. Threatening a collector with a filing is like a quick jab to the nose that carries the risk, cost, and uncertainty of your options. Filing bankruptcy like the two crafty entrepreneurs I mentioned earlier was a preemptive attack on their creditors. When the tides turned, they figured out how to leave someone else holding the bag. Bankruptcy is most often used as a defensive weapon (a shield) by the debtor to get relief from its creditors. Like a handgun, sometimes just the sight of it is enough to get your point across, without having to deal with messy consequences. But to make this sort of threat effectively, you need to retain legal counsel who knows what they're doing and who has the chops to execute, if necessary. Otherwise the threat will ring hollow.

All these considerations regarding Chapter 11 can best be summed up by the simple notion that if you are playing ball on your toes, you'll see lots of options and control the outcome. If you're playing on your heels, you're going to lose. Too many bankruptcies are filed reflexively or out of desperation rather than strategically. That is why Chapter 11 restructurings typically have a 70% chance of failure. Competent Chapter 11 counsel (who have the luxury of time) will draft the plan of reorganization and size up all the parties before they ever push the button to file the case.

Bankruptcy at its core is about disclosing to the world the machinations of your business and revealing all the mistakes you have made – so it takes fortitude. If done correctly, you will maintain control of your assets and business and ultimately restructure your balance sheet to create an entity that can bring value to your stakeholders, including equity. However, there are dozens of pitfalls that can leave you surrendering control and leading to liquidation. You prepare lengthy schedules of every single entity the business owes money to and every single asset with which those creditors might get paid. It sounds clinical and it is. As an entrepreneur it used to be you and, well, everyone else. It was you on the top of the hill and your employees, customers, and vendors all there cheering for you. In bankruptcy it's you but on a medical examination table being poked and prodded by clinicians in what can feel like a very humiliating manner. You need a talented surgeon to take you through to the other side.

The Players

Like a game of chess, bankruptcy has many different "pieces," each with limited moves and limited powers playing in the same forum. Understanding who's in the game, whose side they're on, and what they can do to you is critical and confusing. In the bankruptcy auction for the assets of retailer Smith & Hawkin, a very well positioned strategic buyer backed out of the bidding saying, "I'm not comfortable being here. Being in this courtroom is like being in Middle Earth. All of you folks know each other and speak this mysterious language that only you can understand." As you'll see later in this chapter, it's not nearly that confusing.

In my own bankruptcy I just followed along and never really knew what was happening for two reasons: (1) my brains were scrambled after Hurricane Katrina and my financial collapse, and (2) I let my lawyer "make it easy" for me and just followed along without studying the game and figuring out how to win. I had options, lots of options that were never presented to me, and I never went and unearthed them on my own. So, here's who's showing up:

- **Debtor in Possession (DIP).** This is current owner-ship/management – you if you are the entrepreneur. In the first instance, the debtor acts as his or her own trustee and has relative control over the case. Prepetition management stays in possession (control) of the business. They have first crack at a turnaround plan and 120 days to present it to the court. Sometimes this is a good thing, and sometimes management is the problem.

- **Secured Creditors.** Secured creditors are usually a bank or other prepetition lenders. They have security interest (liens) on the assets (collateral) of the business along with, likely, personal guarantees of the majority owners. Even the third or fourth lender to a business is likely to have filed liens and have a secured claim. You will generally have to make arrangements to pay secured creditors some amount during the case, especially if they are oversecured.

- **Unsecured Creditors Committee.** This is a repre-sentative leadership group of vendors and other trade type creditors who have no direct liens on assets. While trade creditors often make up this committee, it can also contain bondholders and tort claims. The committee is appointed by the U.S. Trustee's Office to represent the collective interests of the unsecured creditors. The opinions of the committee generally carry a lot of weight with the bankruptcy judge, and the committee, surprisingly, can be constituted of your adversaries who pushed you into the Chapter 11 corner.

- **Equity Holders Committee.** The shareholders of the business. If there is a wide ownership structure, then they may elect a committee to represent their joint interests. If ownership is just a few people, they will not need a committee.

- **Ad Hoc Committees.** These committees are anyone else who feels they need a voice. Common examples are bond holders, shareholders, tort, future claimants, and junior debt.

- **Parties to Executory Contracts and Unexpired Leases.** An executory contract is one in which the terms are to be completed at a future date, so it is largely an unperformed contract, though with real damages under a breach. Leases work in a similar fashion and are often the crux issue in a retail bankruptcy. To "assume" a lease in Chapter 11, you must first cure it by paying all amounts due prepetition.

- **The Examiner.** This is a professional appointed by the bankruptcy court to investigate and report the activities of the business to the court. These are only appointed as a fall back and with cause. In the first instance, the debtor controls the ship. In a filing that is surrounded by accusations of fraud, an examiner will be given specific instructions to investigate all irregularities and possible solutions.

- **Chapter 11 Trustee.** Like an examiner, a Chapter 11 trustee only comes on the scene when the debtor has fallen down on the job. This person is appointed by the U.S. Trustee Program to administer the bankruptcy. They gather, manage, liquidate, and account for the assets of the debtor while paying bills and administering the costs of the bankruptcy. They are infrequently used in Chapter 11 filings. Trustees have a financial incentive, called the trustee commission to collect on and liquidate assets for the creditors. The current formula is a sliding scale that rewards the trustee for his or her work:

25% of the first $5,000;

10% of the next $45,000;

5% of the next $950,000; and

3% of the balance.

A debtor can often feel held hostage by this incentive and many feel they have been unfairly squeezed out of protected assets when given the option of settling or the long, painful grind of being investigated by the Bankruptcy Trustee.

- **The U.S. Trustee.** The United States Trustee's Office is part of the U.S. Department of Justice. The office is separate from the court and a watchdog agency charged with monitoring bankruptcy cases, identifying fraud, and supervising all trustees. They take a more active role when no creditors' committee has been appointed – they fall into the role of protecting unsecured creditors. The U.S. Trustee's office will review all petitions and pleadings in the case and participate in some proceedings.

The U.S. Trustee's office can file motions to dismiss the case (awful for the debtor) or to convert a case from, say, a Chapter 11 reorganization to a Chapter 7 liquidation (game over). The U.S. Trustee's office charges quarterly fees to the estate during the course of the bankruptcy.

- **The Bankruptcy Court.** The bankruptcy courts are subject matter jurisdiction units of federal district courts, which have original and exclusive jurisdiction over all bankruptcy cases. Most proceedings are held before a U.S. bankruptcy judge who serves a 14-year term after appointment by the U.S. Court of Appeals in that circuit. Judges typically don't take active roles in cases, but only respond to filings made by these various constituents. One judge likened their role to being in a closet at a party – you have an idea of what's happening, but only get a clear picture when someone opens to the door to ask you to resolve a dispute.

- **Powerful Government Agencies.** This includes; IRS, EPA, DOL who will not be deterred by your bankruptcy filing. Generally, don't mess with wages, payroll taxes, retirement trust funds, or environmental issues. They will follow you right into court and, surprise, these federal agencies have a loud voice in this federal court.

When you review the list of players one thought should sink in; you are completely outgunned, which is why you need an excellent bankruptcy attorney and a path, and why you need to be entirely tuned in to the process.

The Professional Team

People wonder why bankruptcy costs are so high? Here's why.

- **Lawyers, lots of lawyers.** Your regular old commercial lawyer and his litigation partner is going to tag along while you pay a corporate bankruptcy lawyer top dollar. Like a cardiologist, these guys are billing at the top of the food chain, regardless of location. Bankruptcy attorneys work feverishly to prepare a filing and administer it through the early exciting and contentious days of a filing.

- **"Ordinary course" professionals.** You still need your CPA, your tax attorney, and maybe your outsourced CFO.

- **Valuation experts.** As you'll see, the successful way out of bankruptcy is driven by the valuation of the business. You'll have your experts, the creditors will have theirs, and then the lawyers and valuation experts will argue about who is right – all on the company's dime. It's easy to have 10 high-dollar professionals debating for hours the value of the business, but the final path forward will be set in these discussions, so it is critically important.

- **Accountants.** There are lots and lots of accountants auditing backward and forward to make sure everything is pinned down and explained. The bankruptcy process is driven by the transparency of accurate numbers, so accountants are at the core of it all.

- **Financial advisors.** In larger cases, financial advisors might be a firm that specializes in restructuring bonds or commercial debts. In businesses under $50 million, you might have one consultant doing the restructuring, selling, and fixing of the business all at the same time.

- **Investment bankers.** Perhaps we've entered a Chapter 11 intending to sell the business through a 363 bankruptcy sale process. We'll need sell-side advisors with experience marketing distressed business through quick and efficient bidding.

- **Turnaround consultants.** Turnaround consultants are the professionals managing the cash flow and daily operations of the business, while also crafting and executing the turnaround and restructuring plan to fix the business and set it up for long-term future success.

- **Auctioneers.** One of the first auctions I ever managed had a used Toyota pickup truck that everyone blue book valued at $16,000. The auctioneer opened bidding at $14,000 to pull people in. No one bid. He dropped to $13,500 – nothing. $13,000 – nothing. $10,000 – nothing. He dropped down all the way to $3,000 before capturing the first bid. Then slowly, incrementally he brought in others and created momentum. The bids were gathering steam as they roared passed the initial opening value of $14,000 and past the blue book value of $16,000. The maestro whipped the bidders into a glorious overvalued crescendo peaking with the final bid at $17,700. For thousands of years, auctions have been the most efficient and effective way of deriving full value from assets in a completely public and transparent manner. Auctioneers are also appraisers and help creditors establish a worst-case liquidation value.

Funding a Bankruptcy

Bankruptcies are funded either by cash reserves, internally generated cash flow, cash infusion, or from loans. A company that can internally fund a bankruptcy likely has a strong income statement and an overburdened balance sheet. The purpose of this filing would be to haircut the debt and give this well-performing business a right-sized balance sheet. Companies for which both the income statement and balance sheet need repair are harder to save, and the law only gives you 120 days to create a good plan, with some exceptions. Before filing, you must ensure that if you put aside legacy debt, the business will cash flow. If not, don't waste your time. Additionally, you've got to finance this period of time while paying absurd professional fees.

Loans are possible and they are called debtor in possession (DIP) loans. They enter the debt stack at superpriority position, above all other creditors provided the secured creditors agree to be subordinated. It seems like a pretty big ask for management to tell creditors: "We obviously screwed up but we're going to subordinate you so we can take on even more debt and we've got 120 days to come up with a plan." But the courts allow it because, like the railroad, the possibility of a going concern has the greatest value to all stakeholders. Likewise, the incumbent senior secured lender is free to offer that DIP loan if they wish to increase their position. Another interesting tension in bankruptcies is that creditors may safely recover their value through a liquidation, whereas equity holders must pursue risk to recover their value.

It would be hard and rare for a business with revenues under $50 million to attract a DIP lender. Below that volume, a business without positive cash flow or significant cash reserves is unlikely to survive a bankruptcy. They will struggle to secure financing, and the base costs of a filing will be disproportionally high to their revenue base. A company that enters weak can be converted to a liquidation by an aggressive creditor. Bigger filings with very secure assets (say a critical parts supplier to Boeing) will attract banks and bank type lenders who simply want a fair return on conservative risk. Filings with less secure assets, like a consumer brand company, will attract "sharkier" type investors including loan-to-own investors who simply want an outsized return for their higher degree of risk and/or to wrestle control of the company away from the owners.

Bankruptcy is a safe harbor for beleaguered businesses. A company can file a Chapter 11, get immediate relief from creditors, and have time to formulate a plan and marshal resources before facing up to its debts. Figure 7.3 illustrates the restructuring options facing a troubled business along with the Chapter 11 process.

Activities in bankruptcy proceedings are particularly intense at the start and end of the process, whereas the many months in between are focused primarily on running the company and administering the bankruptcy. If you're lucky, it is all quite mundane. This has been referred to as an inverted bell curve of activity, something I refer to as the Valley of the Grind.

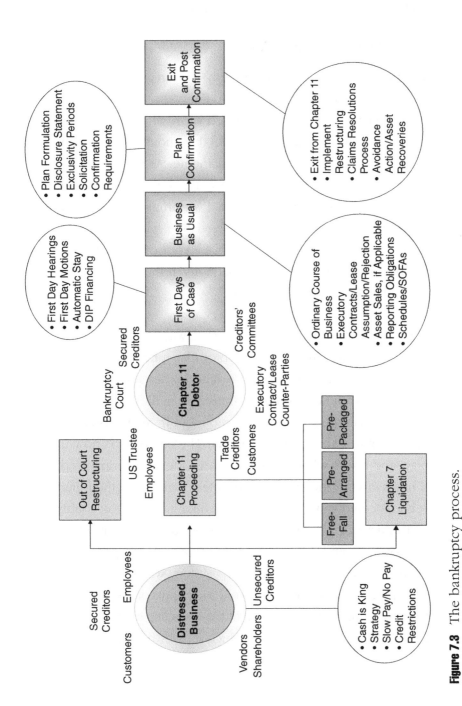

Figure 7.3 The bankruptcy process.

Credit: James H.M. Sprayregen and Jonathan Friedland

Stages of a Bankruptcy Filing

The first stage of a bankruptcy filing is strategy and preparation. A good attorney won't let you file without a really good plan of what you want to accomplish with a filing. Bankruptcy is an expensive and dangerous tool that should only be handled with great forethought and planning. As we lay out the objectives of a filing, perhaps there are ways to accomplish the same results but out of court. Even until the day of filing, your options are open. A negotiation with your largest creditor, in which you bring and place your completely filled out bankruptcy schedules and petitions in the middle of the table, may break a prior impasse.

Stage 2 is the actual filing, which always generates great amounts of excitement as the debtor files a raft of schedules and "first-day" motions, which reveal the heretofore darkest secrets of its finances and operations. Often, these papers hint at the ultimate plan of reorganization, but in many instances, that is not revealed until much later. The company is now in play, and this is when the tables turn for everyone involved. If news of your intentions were to leak out before the filing, vendors could shut off supply, or banks may offset accounts and inflict harm upon the business or customers, or critical employees could get spooked and leave. A company normally files in their state of incorporation, which is immediately part of the public record and picked up on news feeds. However, unlike filing choices in business litigation, a debtor can file in any jurisdiction in which it does business, giving the filer broad opportunity to forum or judge shop. Most big cases end up in Delaware or New York, both of which have extensive and predictable bodies of case law. Every single creditor will be listed on schedules, and they will immediately begin receiving notices from the bankruptcy court advising them of the filing. To receive anything beyond the original filing, however, one must file an "appearance" in the case and should do so immediately. When the secret is finally released, the news will ripple through all levels of the community. Your employees will be shocked, and the bank may be caught off-guard by a filing. Communities in which your suppliers live may will be affected. As an entrepreneur, the searing light of transparency will shine on you, but if you are a crafty capitalist, this may all be part of a well-orchestrated business strategy.

Filings are made online these days, and the file is time stamped when received by the court. All debt incurred before that moment is now suspended and will be administered through this process. An automatic stay is statutorily imposed by the bankruptcy code, as the name implies, automatically. This means that all creditors must immediately stop all collection, foreclosure, and eviction activities. Even if they were in the process of repossessing your delivery trucks, they have to stop or revert back to that very minute when the filing was made. Even government agencies, with some exceptions, must stop and adhere to the rules of bankruptcy. This includes IRS collection efforts but does not include police powers of arrest or, perhaps, EPA-type enforcement.

With the filing comes the first-day motions in which the company petitions the court for things like:

- The ability to pay prepetition employee wages, because no one wants employees upset when trying to maintain value in the business. Prepetition and prefiling mean the same thing.

- The ability to maintain current bank accounts and cash-management procedures.

- The ability to use the cash collateral in the business to fund ongoing operations.

- The ability to hire attorneys and other insolvency professionals.

- Perhaps the ability to pay certain critical vendors some or all of their prepetition debt.

These are often approved temporarily on an ex-parte basis (with only a limited hearing). Motions approved by the court become first-day orders, which allow management some flexibility within the statutory prohibitions of the bankruptcy code. The debtor group is expected to attend hearings on the first-day motions while also communicating with employees, customers, creditors, investors, and maybe even the press. The debtor will also meet with the office of the U.S. Trustee and prepare exhaustive schedules for the court.

In these initial days, the U.S. Trustee will attempt to form a creditor's committee and possibly other committees with wide ability to watch over the debtor business and participate in the forming of the reorganization plan. With court approval, the creditor's committee may hire an attorney and other professionals. This is the debtor's time to shine. The more convincing management can be that they have a good plan, the more support they will receive. Committees are generally not the friend of the debtor, and to some extent they can be avoided through communication with these constituents prior to or immediately after the case is filed. If parties trust you, they'll give you some rope to run things – for a time.

The third phase of a bankruptcy case is the long middle part where the business runs in a somewhat ordinary course of business. Vendors are paid promptly, shipments are made, employees are paid, and so on. There will continue to be deadlines and required filings and an occasional dust up as creditors comment on past or present management decisions. If creditors don't like how the company is managed in the turnaround, they can petition the court with their suggestions. If they feel certain parties were unfairly paid in the months leading up to the filing, creditors can request the debtor to seek avoidance of prior payments and "clawback" or "disgorge" those funds back to the estate. This means undoing the transfer through force of the court. The debtor is motivated to accumulate the greatest possible pool of assets for the benefit of its reorganization efforts.

Payments or transfers are usually avoided (reversed and recovered) for one of three reasons:

1. **Fraudulent transfer,** like selling company assets really cheap to your brother in the months or even years leading up to a filing. The court will force him

to return those goods at their value and it will be an unpleasant experience for him to do so. There is a two year look-back period under bankruptcy law for such transfers, and in some states this period is up to four years.

2. **Preference.** The court assumes the debtor was considering bankruptcy for 90 days before the actual filing and may have made moves to advantage certain creditors over others and in direct contradiction to the absolute priority of debt rules. The court expects to see that creditors were paid in an even way over the months preceding a filing. If one or two creditors were paid outsized amounts, then those payments will be investigated. If, say, the payment was COD for steel to supply an extraordinarily large shipment, then that is a "normal course" transaction and may not be avoided. If vendor payables are all stretched an average of 60 days but one gets paid off in full, leading up to the filing, well that smells fishy and will likely be "avoided." Meaning the court will force the vendor to return those payments.

It's the timing and amount of payment that stands out, not so much the legitimacy of it during insolvency. If payments are standard and part of the business operations over a long period of time, then they will be considered "ordinary course" and not extraordinary. I know a situation in which the entrepreneur was having the company pay $10,000 per month for years into the (bankruptcy exempt) cash value of his life insurance policy. When hard times came and the bank scrutinized expenses, this was never objected to, likely because it was buried in the Insurance line on the income statement. The company eventually failed and filed Chapter 7, but those payments were made right up until the actual wind-down, allowing the 100% founder/owner to keep all that cash value.

3. **Strong-arm powers (actual name).** This clause gives the trustee special powers to "avoid" (get rid of) certain liens and unperfected security interests. Assets like real estate or big mills may have unperfected mechanics liens. Or the company borrowed from a wealthy uncle and the loan agreement clearly states a second lien on named assets but the wealthy uncle's attorney forgot to file the proper paperwork to register that lien. These are creditors who do not have a voice at the table and whom the debtor or a trustee can just wipe out to clear the deck for the creditors who do have supportable claims.

Early in the middle period of the case, the debtor will be required to attend a first meeting of creditors in which the debtor company's representative will answer questions to the U.S. Trustee and perhaps creditors under oath. The debtor will also have to meet in private with the U.S. Trustee in what's called an initial debtor interview where the U.S. Trustee's financial analyst will inquire about the inner financial workings of the business and the anticipated plan. Creditors then begin submitting proofs of claim, which may later be allowed or opposed by the debtor.

This long middle path is overrun with distractions, which can easily get a CEO unfocused on the goal of successfully exiting the company from bankruptcy. A real danger during this period is a lack of change, and it is incumbent on the debtor's professionals and other constituents to ensure it's not just business as usual – real restructuring needs to occur. Segregation of duties is the best way forward. The CEO should be head-down focused on the business while professionals deal with the sorted administrative and legal encumbrances encountered along the way.

Phase 4 is the exit from bankruptcy. This requires a plan that creditors vote on and must be approved by the court. As we'll see in Chapter 8, Debt Restructuring, bankruptcy is little more than a big complicated way of negotiating your debts with creditors, with referees. The company has to offer everyone a good enough deal based on the fundamental recovery power of the business. While out of court, angry creditors can refuse a good deal and continue to harass you; in bankruptcy they need to sit still until they either agree to a deal or one is "crammed down" upon them by a majority vote of creditors. Each creditor class is resolved by majority acceptance of the plan (>50% in number and >two-thirds in the dollar amount of claims) and all creditor classes need to be either made whole or resolved before the plan can be confirmed and the company is released from bankruptcy.

Prepackaged bankruptcies are becoming more and more common, especially among more experienced filers. Also referred to as free fall, pre-arranged, or prepack, these are bankruptcy filings that have been so thoroughly orchestrated that the creditors are already on board and support management in the plan. This way the filing sails through the process and, in theory, gets a quick confirmation of plan and release on the other side. On the surface, getting your creditors to all accept a haircut without the hammer of bankruptcy seems like a really tough task but often they are highly motivated to see the company survive. Here are three situations I can think of offhand in which a prepack might make sense:

1. If I'm a turnaround investor and I find a business with the following maladies: the supply chain is locking up, customer orders are late, the company supplies critical limited-supply parts or services to big companies, and the problems seem fixable. Without help, the current path will lead to some critical vendor cutting them off, which will create a domino effect resulting in an unfunded payroll and the total collapse of the business within weeks to months. This is the equivalent of a vendor repossessing his two miles of railroad track. I might be clever enough to gather the customers, vendors, and employees together and paint a better picture – one in which we all hold hands and save the business for the benefit of all. You can liquidate the meager assets now and maybe the only one who gets paid is the bank; vendor debt gets completely hosed, employees lose their jobs, and customers have big issues without supply. But if we support the company, the bank can remain protected while vendors can receive partial payments from future cash flows and customers and employees are very happy. We all agree and formalize it through an expedited (prepack) Chapter 11. This provides the cleanest

possible (most legally certain) way of transferring in assets and locks in commitments.

This sort of prepack sale of substantially all the assets happens under section 363 of the bankruptcy code. Today many Chapter 11s are filed with the goal of simply selling the assets through an expedited auction process where a bidder agrees to allow his offer to be bid against – known as a stalking horse bidder. The stalking horse bidder is afforded certain financial remuneration if he is outbid. Generally, the sale price has to cover the level of secured debt only, and the buyer will take the assets free and clear of any and all claims, including unfavorable worker's compensation mod rates. Often, 363 sales are entirely engineered prior to the filing, then quickly approved by the Court. Frequently, all that's left is the bidding.

2. Think of the GM or Chrysler bankruptcies; those were largely precoordinated and set records both for size and speed of plan confirmation. Over time, Chapter 11s had grown lengthy, cumbersome, and expensive. By the mid-2000s it was not unusual for a Chapter 11 to take 18 months and need to fund preposterously high professional fees. In 2009–2010 a postfinancial crisis wave of bankruptcies hit the courts and overwhelmed them. The courts applied direct pressure to attorneys and have both cut attorney billing rates and sped up the process considerably. GM and Chrysler are prime examples.

3. Asbestos claims have driven many companies through an arranged bankruptcy even if it wasn't done in the modern prepack fashion. When a healthy company gets

hit with a massive lawsuit (unsecured claim), it can suddenly owe an amount that defies math but makes sense only to a jury or government regulator. This can be seen as an attack on all the stakeholders of a business – owners, customers, vendors, and employees – which makes unifying their defense much easier.

Plan of Reorganization: Six-Step Process

1. Negotiating the plan with major constituencies.

2. Drafting the plan of reorganization and the disclosure statement.

3. Getting court approval for the disclosure statement.

4. Solicitation process with creditors who are "impaired" or not made whole through the reorganization.

5. Confirmation hearing.

6. Performing to the plan.

You'll see that this requires a bit of shuttle diplomacy. The debtor must get stakeholder consent for a plan, then build out that plan, then get the court to approve the plan, then get the stakeholders to vote on the plan, and then get the court to confirm that vote.

All this starts with a well-defined exit plan, which is developed by the debtor within the 120-day exclusivity period. If the debtor fails to develop a successful plan (or get the court to grant extensions, which it prefers to do less of these days), then other parties can suggest plans. This is a distinct debtor advantage to the U.S. bankruptcy system because the debtor has plentiful opportunity to control the process.

The plan of reorganization should ideally detail structural and management changes to the business and then forecast the impact of those changes through the standard financial statements. The plan will also show the balance sheet impact of: asset sales, divestitures, shutting down divisions, debt to equity conversions or reverse, equity issuance or cancellation, restructuring debts through principle, amortization, and/or interest rate, as well as all the attendant legal matters such as adjustments to liens, curing or waiving defaults, and changes in corporate governance or structure.

Think of the disclosure statement as being similar to the details buried in the prospectus of a financial investment package. In effect, you are offering debts and equity in a renovated company for a prescribed amount of money. Interestingly, you will not need to comply with Securities and Exchange Commission (SEC) regulations that might cover this sort of offering because bankruptcy is a safe-harbor from SEC-type rules. It's not unusual for a disclosure statement to exceed 50 pages as it reestablishes all creditor claims and classes plus assets. The plan meticulously describes how each piece or class of collateral will be used to satisfy the claims upon them, detailing the percentage net recovery for each creditor or creditor class. The statement will cover voting rules, risk factors, feasibility, liquidation analysis, tax consequences, and perhaps even multiple payout options for the plan. Once prepared, the plan and disclosure statement are submitted to the court for its approval.

Like everything else in life, the entire bankruptcy restructuring process requires salesmanship. The debtors and their professionals will need to persuade each creditor or creditor class (and their professionals) that this is the best possible recovery from a crummy situation and earn their support while the plan is being constructed. The debtors will need to carry that support through the process and manage their creditors who may want to lash out at the debtor. If a class of creditors is paid in full, then those creditors are satisfied and there is no need for them to vote. However, if the creditors are required to restructure their debt in any little way, then they are "impaired" and thus entitled to vote, ideally in favor of the plan. It is only impaired (not fully satisfied) classes who get to vote their approval of the plan. For approval, a creditor class needs support of a majority by number of creditors in that class and two-thirds support of the creditor dollars owed. There is the possibility that a creditor class will refuse the debtor's offer and seek to hold up the entire exit. Without a better alternative, the court may "cram-down" or force the dissenting creditors to accept the offer on the grounds that other creditor classes have, and the solution is seen as better than a Chapter 7 liquidation. This is why you'll often see trade creditors receive maybe 10% recovery even though, mathematically, they should have been out of the money. The 10% may be an offering from the senior creditors as the juniors are forced/persuaded to accept the plan. Again, it all comes down to the strength of the reorganization plan. It is required to exit a bankruptcy, and the court will often go out of its way to protect a good plan, because they are a rare and valuable thing when every other option is carnage.

A successful restructuring offers what no other insolvency outcome does – namely, the prospect of future cash flows.

So while a liquidation feeds a few quickly (and destroys a community), a reorganization feeds many slowly and protects economic vitality. With future cash flows, low-ranking creditors can be paid out over time, and the family loan can be converted to equity and benefit through their continued support of the business.

The following pro forma income statement (Figure 7.4) shows a company which declined in 2017 and filed Chapter 11 later in that year. With support from creditors and customers,

Income Statement	2016	2017 TTM	Forecast 2018	Forecast 2019	Forecast 2020	Forecast 2021	Forecast 2022
Revenues	10,000	8,000	9,000	9,500	10,000	10,500	11,000
COGS	6,500	5,600	5,850	6,175	6,500	6,825	7,150
GPM $	3,500	2,400	3,150	3,325	3,500	3,675	3,850
GPM %	35.0%	30.0%	35.0%	35.0%	35.0%	35.0%	35.0%
SGA	3,500	3,500	3,000	3,000	3,000	3,000	3,000
Operating Profit (cash)	–	(1,100)	150	325	500	675	850
Debt Service	500	500	50	100	150	175	200
Net Cash	(500)	(1,600)	100	225	350	500	650
Cumulative Cash Recovery			–	225	575	1,075	1,725

Figure 7.4 Pro forma income statement showing future cash flows for servicing debt and building equity.

the business can restructure its debts, stretching some out while haircutting others, cut costs, and reenergize the business. This creates future cash flows to service the ongoing debts and provide long-term value to all stakeholders.

Future cash flows are not balance sheet items, meaning they can only service debt if the business can be made profitable. That is why a successful restructuring, no matter how deep the losses are, is usually preferred over a liquidation. Figure 7.5 represents these future cash flows and shows a significantly higher recovery in a successful Chapter 11 reorganization compared to a Chapter 7 liquidation. In this situation, two more classes of creditors receive a full recovery, a third class receives a partial recovery, and the family loan is converted to equity. Not illustrated are the cash-flow benefits from stretching out the company's debts.

With votes solicited, the debtor goes back to the court for confirmation of its plan based on satisfying the following 14 requirements:

1. The plan and plan proponent are both in compliance with the Bankruptcy Code.

2. The plan was developed in good faith.*

3. Bankruptcy Court approves the accrued payments to professionals.

4. The plan provides full disclosure and identity of post-confirmation officers and directors.*

5. Regulatory approval if required.

ACME Mfg. – Value Preservation in a Reorganization

Account	Book Value	Chapter 7 Liquidation	Chapter 11 Recovery
Cash	–	–	–
Accounts Receivable	1,000	800	900
Inventory	2,500	625	1,800
Total Current Assets	**3,500**	**1,425**	**2,700**
Machinery and Equipment (net)	1,800	1,200	1,200
Intellectual Property	500	20	100
Furniture and Fixtures	200	–	40
Computers and Software (net)	700	10	140
Leasehold Improvements (net)	800	–	–
Goodwill (net)	1,300	–	
Bankruptcy Admin Fees		(200)	(500)
Value of Future Cash Flows			1,725
Total Long-Term Assets	**5,300**	**1,030**	**2,705**
Total Assets	**8,800**	**2,455**	**5,405**
Recoveries in Priority Rank			
First Bank Revolver	2,100	2,100	2,100
First Bank Term Note, SBA backed	1,500	355	1,500
Second Bank – Cash Advance Loan	250		250
State BDC Loan, no PG	100		100
Family Loan	1,000		
Accounts Payable	1,500		1,200
Total Recoveries	**6,450**	**2,655**	**5,150**
	Recovery	38%	80%
Equity	**2,350**	**0**	**255**

Figure 7.5 Improvement in creditor recovery through a successful reorganization.

6. Best interest of creditors test, which requires a result better than liquidation. Otherwise, a liquidation is in the best interest of creditors.

7. The plan is consensual.

8. The plan provides specific treatment of administrative and priority claims.

9. Prohibition on complete "cram-down" plans, there needs to be some levels of support.

10. Feasibility.*

11. Payment of court, filing, and US Trustee fees.

12. The plan protects retiree benefits.

13. The plan treats transfers to not-for-profit entities properly.

14. The plan and the filing are not simply a ruse to avoid taxes.

With the necessary votes of creditors and confirmation by the court, the company exits bankruptcy court with a clean slate. Although there may be some emotional overhang, there is no/none/zero trailing liability exposure. Short of fraud, it is impossible for a bankruptcy process to be unwound or revisited. It is legally impenetrable, which provides the greatest possible comfort to participants and is part of bankruptcy's appeal.

---

*Most likely points of contention between debtor and creditor.

The Stigma of Bankruptcy

Years ago, when I was contemplating my own bankruptcy, an attorney in New Orleans told me that in certain industries bankruptcy can be seen as a badge of honor. In a slow southern drawl he said, "Hell, in the oil business if you don't have at least one bankruptcy under your belt people won't think you've been trying very hard."

Although I don't know the individual backstories, here is a list of famous people who have filed for bankruptcy protection: Abraham Lincoln, Charles Goodyear (tires), Daniel Defoe (Robinson Crusoe), George Fredric Handel (composer), Henry Ford, James Wilson (Supreme Court Justice), Milton Hershey, Oscar Wilde, Oskar Schindler (Schindler's List), Rembrandt, Samuel Clemens (Mark Twain), Thomas Paine, Ulysses S. Grant, Walt Disney, William McKinley (25th president), and Donald Trump (45th American president).[1]

Well-known companies that have survived through bankruptcy include General Motors, Chrysler, Dunkin Donuts, Samsonite, Mrs. Fields, the Chicago Cubs, Gibson Guitars, Pacific Gas & Electric, Delta Airlines, American Airlines, United Airlines, US Airways, Air Canada, and many others.

When Should You Throw in the Towel?

It is rarely clear how long you should fight to stave off bankruptcy or when you should just give in and focus on recovery. Logically, giving in might be the best option, but accepting failure and moving on has a high emotional cost that can stay with you for years.

Emotional Argument – Never file bankruptcy; the regret will tear you up and eat you alive. I've given this speech to clients but I believe it in my soul; I would rather be Cool Hand Luke standing back up to get knocked down again and again than to live with the years of regret. I would torch the whole village – dogs, cats, children – to avoid going through that again. I did it totally wrong and ended up on the very short end of the stick, and the regret has been a burden to bear. I wouldn't recommend bankruptcy to anyone.

Financial Argument – A reasonable rule of thumb that if you can't conceivably pay off your extraordinary debts in five years, then you should consider a bankruptcy filing. It's a reasonable measure, and bankruptcy does give you the certainty of release and a clean slate. There is also some satisfaction of flipping the bird to certain creditors as you grit your teeth and file. You'll drag that clean slate of bankruptcy around like an anchor for 10 years while it's on your credit report, but most of those issues can be solved with creativity. This financial argument also denies the possibility of restructuring your debts out of court, which is usually possible. Every so often, even a logical restructuring is impossible because your creditor simply wants to push you off a cliff. If that's the case and you're trapped with no way out, then you simply need to switch to defense, re-arrange your assets (legally), put on your helmet, file the bankruptcy and take the hits.

Reorganization Out of Court

I once had an investment banker tell me that he had referred three distressed clients to bankruptcy attorneys and each time the client ended up filing bankruptcy. "And now," he said, "I'm wondering if that's just what bankruptcy attorneys do? Like the hammer who sees every problem as a nail?" For some attorneys the answer is yes, they are one-trick ponies. For an entrepreneur, I suggest an attorney with both legitimate bankruptcy and litigation experience, someone who can fairly advise you of your full range of options, both in and out of court. Also check their backstory as it may reveal character and drive. One excellent bankruptcy attorney in upstate New York experienced her parents' bankruptcy as a child and she is a bit of a caped-crusader, trying to protect others from similar loss. A good friend, who has become a federal bankruptcy judge, had his own entrepreneurial roller coaster ride with his family-owned restaurant. After a few years of ups and downs, they sold the restaurant, and, although it didn't make him wealthy, it certainly made him a better bankruptcy attorney and judge.

Everything we just covered in this chapter provides the backstop against what you negotiate out-of-court settlements with. Said another way, bankruptcy is the anvil against which out-of-court settlements are established and what we cover in the following chapter.

Note

1. http://www.bankruptcylawhelp.com/Bankruptcy/Famous-People-Who-Filed-Bankruptcy.aspx.

Chapter 8

Debt Restructuring Out of Court

Bankruptcy law is the anvil on which out-of-court restructurings are hammered out. What we just explored in the prior chapter on bankruptcy is the most expensive, uncertain, and feared debt restructuring alternative in the United States – and it's not that bad. You get the full chess board with all the pieces and you have 120 days to make most of the moves. And when complete, you get the world's strongest formal release of debts.

Simplistically, an out-of-court restructuring mirrors the bankruptcy process but without all the indignities of court orders and begging permission for simple business decisions; also, without much of the cost, reputational tarnish, or the perceived risks associated with bankruptcy. If run properly, the restructuring will track the bankruptcy process and be above reproach in its methodology. This approach defends the restructuring process from lawsuits during its development and afterward, should someone try to unravel a consensual restructuring.

The biggest risk to an out-of-court restructuring is that several creditors (even small ones buried in the debt stack) can band together and declare war on your process. Although bankruptcy issues an automatic stay to collection efforts, there is no similar protection out of court. If you're working out payment arrangements for unsecured creditors to get paid 70% now or 100% over two years, all your vendors will probably support it because they want to keep you as a customer, raise prices a bit, and collect most of their money, and certainly all of their costs. But someone who's never going to work with you again has no ulterior future benefit and may want to be aggressive and force payment in full.

Several collection lawsuits can start draining your resources and could even make your incomplete restructuring now unaffordable because these collection attacks are costing so much to defend or pay off.

The strongest defense against all this is the debtor's threat to seek relief in a Chapter 11. That threat usually creates a long pause in the conversation with the creditor. Once someone on our side glibly brings up our willingness to file for Chapter 11, the conversation shifts out of their control. We know everything about bankruptcy and they know very little. We have been developing this alternative for months and will control the process in or out of court. Everything we have done in our restructuring process has lead us to this exact point; we are fully prepared to present this exact same plan in court and have the result forced upon these rogue creditors. We end the conversation saying that if they would like to retain their own bankruptcy counsel, we are happy to share a copy of our filing paperwork, which we've prepared in advance of this conversation.

So, with knowledge of the bankruptcy code and confidence in your methods, you can move on to restructuring your debts. Twenty percent of what remains is math, 70% is persuasion, and maybe 10% legal work. Just as in bankruptcy, we'll have to show how restructuring is the vastly superior outcome to the risk of bankruptcy and that a Chapter 11 might convert to a liquidating Chapter 7.

I often lead with a liquidation analysis as I find it can stop many belligerent creditors in their tracks and help others understand just how poorly a liquidation will work for them. Liquidation values change over time and were at a historical low in 2009 during the global financial crisis. Figure 8.1 shows approximate values during two recent time periods.

Your bank will favor an out-of-court settlement since they are at the top of the debt stack and don't need the cost or slow pace of bankruptcy to establish that fact. In the right circumstances they might support a bankruptcy if it will protect

ACME Mfg. - Liquidation Values Over Time			
		2017	2009
	Book	Liquidation	Liquidation
Account	Value	Value	Value
Cash	-	-	
Accounts Receivable	1,000	800	500
Inventory	2,500	625	400
Total Current Assets	**3,500**	**1,425**	**900**
Machinery & Equipment (net)	1,800	1,200	600
Intellectual Property	500	20	-
Furniture & Fixtures	200	-	-
Computers & software (net)	700	10	-
Leasehold Improvements (net)	800	-	-
Goodwill (net)	1,300	-	-
Total Long-term Assets	**5,300**	**1,230**	**600**
Total Assets	**8,800**	**2,655**	**1,500**
	% recovery	30%	17%

Figure 8.1 Liquidation values over time.

them and help the company wipe out pesky, nonstrategic debt lower down the pecking order. Your unsecureds are usually out of the money or severely impaired (coming up short) making them inclined to accept the logic of avoiding an expensive filing, leaving more money for them.

What you won't have outside of bankruptcy is protection from creditors. You'll have to deal with the big serious ones and learn to handle the small pesky ones.

Corporate Collections

Everyone knows that an LLC is a limited liability company and it really is just that, it limits your liability through a company, just as an S or C Corp limits your personal liability. So when your company buys goods and services on credit (company purchase order, invoices addressed to company, company payment history, etc.) and then one day your company can't pay, it's the company that is responsible, not shareholders. Only when you have either personally guaranteed the debt, provided your social security number on the application, or have acted fraudulently can they come after you personally.

Anyone who understands the liability of a personal guarantee should know exactly if and when they have signed one. It's generally in your mortgage, your bank loan, your credit cards, and likely other loans, and definitely in Small Business Administration (SBA) loans. Any credit application where you provided your social security number was underwritten on your personal credit.

Even without a personal guarantee, many corporate collection agencies will go right at the entrepreneur, making them feel personally liable for the debts. This works because entrepreneurs, especially the smaller, less sophisticated ones identify with their business and its debts personally. An effective method of collecting is to go right for the throat and scare the business owner into paying. These collectors are paid on commission, so they have every motivation to separate you from your money. Although their collections would likely be reversed in a bankruptcy, it's a transient industry and they're moving through lists as quickly as they can.

There are two types of collection efforts: internal and third party. Internal collectors are generally the AR clerk of your supplier, who has supported you for years and is a partner and lender to your business. These folks are mostly well-intended employees who work for a business like yours. As nicely and informatively as I can, I explain where they are in the debt stack, what's happening with the bank, and how we need to keep product moving to support the business. "Patience is the key," I tell them. "We got into this mess slowly and the only thing that can happen quickly at this point is a liquidation."

Third-party collectors are new to the scene. They have not supported your business, they are not a partner or stakeholder or lender to you in any way and they are not rooting for you – they are simply trying to apply pressure and take cash that rightfully belongs to the senior secured creditor. It's an industry and it works. I use collections agencies for my own businesses and find that most are legitimate and conscientious. I also deal with a few hundred collection efforts at each business I manage and I can tell you that the collections industry has worked hard to earn its tarnished reputation. I've taken thousands of collections calls for clients and have had thousands of unique experiences, some with enjoyable yet aggressive collectors and others with dirty, rotten, lying scoundrels.

The key to defending any collection effort is to be seriously and diligently working on a really good plan to save the business and get them paid. The other is to know the law and the absolute priority of debt rule as covered in Chapter 7. Not understanding the debt stack can get you in a bunch of trouble. Not understanding who has leverage over you can be excruciating.

When dealing with collectors, most distressed entrepreneurs burn up their goodwill with naïve promise after naïve promise and have zero leniency left with the trade by the time I get involved. By now, lawsuits are either being threatened or filed. The best way to deal with these collectors is to help them self-select their priority. I get on the phone with a hostile collector and simply explain (remember, all their calls are recorded):

> Yes, your debt is acknowledged; I see it right here on the accounts payable ledger. On the surface, I don't dispute that the debt may be owed by this company, but we'll be doing a thorough audit of payables in the future. Right now, we're prioritizing payments; maybe you can help me out. Tell me, is

your debt secured or unsecured? (If they don't know, try not to laugh and assume it's unsecured). Okay, so unsecured, got it. The next question is determining which lenders in each class will be providing additional working capital in the turnaround and which will not. As you can imagine, those participating move up the debt stack.

The rookie collectors will get flustered and move on to the next call. The more experienced will want to tussle a bit. My suggestion is that you just make it as clean and clinical as you can, following the constructs of Chapter 7 on bankruptcy.

> Them: We're unsecured but we need you to pay in full today or we're filing suit.
>
> Me: This conversation is being recorded, right?
>
> Them: Yes.
>
> Me: Good, then I want to go on record telling you that the company is in workout with its secured creditor who has a first position lien on all assets. The company is insolvent and is not allowed to pay you, by law. If you file suit we will present those same facts and this recorded phone call as evidence that you are wasting the court's time. And further, we need working capital to keep the business running. Our bankruptcy lawyer (the worst thing they can hear) has advised us that through a proper recapitalization, some creditors may be advanced and some may be impaired, so you should bring that message back to your client and see if they prefer to move backward or forward in this process.

> A better plan than the costly litigation you are
> threatening is to call me back in four weeks at
> which time we should have earned a forbearance
> period from the bank and will be in a much better
> position to work on a payment plan for you.

Smooth talking doesn't always work. I know a tough collection attorney that files suit before he even bothers sending a letter. He's as much of a shakedown artist as anything else but his tactics get people's attention.

Before I show up at a new company, it's usually the poor, downtrodden accounts payable clerk who is dealing with these bullying collection calls or it's the stressed-out owner taking the calls, trading his credibility for time. And the less experienced you are, the more aggressive the collectors become, including tactics such as the following:

- "We're sending an asset inspector to your business (horrifying thought if you're a retail business) who will compile a complete list of all the assets for us." The collector will obliquely mention spending time in your town and talking to your neighbors. All you can imagine is IRS-style tactics. Ignore this; they're not sending anyone. Tell them to come visit you personally, that you'll buy them a coffee, and give them a tour of the building. This is a made-up tactic, so it doesn't matter.

- "Mr. Smith we want to know why you are driving an Audi when you owe my client $10,000"? All you can think is: Uh-oh, how do they know what I drive; what else do they know about me? They're doing this to get under your skin. Ignore it. You'd be amazed how these insolvency stories play out; I know a CEO who maintained his chauffeured Mercedes throughout his company's Chapter 11 bankruptcy.

- "I'm at the courthouse steps ready to file suit against you today, unless you wire me a bunch of money." These tactics work best on Friday, or the last day of the month, or on the fifteenth of the month, and so on. They want action, show action: "Okay, you got me. Call my bankruptcy attorney and he will petition the bank for payment on your behalf." That works great, they're not calling your bankruptcy attorney. They're going to hang up and call the next business owner, seeing who they can bully for payments that day.

- "You owe this personally and we're going to sue you personally and get a personal judgement on you and your Audi." Just politely ask them to mail you a copy of the personal guarantee and hang up on them. If they do have a personal guarantee on you, figure out how to pay them. Otherwise, put on your helmet and get ready to take some hits.

- "We're going to call your bank and tell them you're not paying your bills. It's First National, right?" This is good psychological warfare, it really gets under a business owner's skin. Don't confirm the bank name but let them know that your bank has you in workout and that the bank, IRS, and your bankruptcy attorney all understand the difficulty your business has had recently. They are not calling your bank and no workout officer cares what an unsecured creditor has to say so they wouldn't return the call anyway.

- In extreme cases, they will find out where you live and call neighbors or family members. Or if you are in a small town, they will call people with the same last name leaving messages that they are looking for John Smith who owes us $10,000. And yes, your spouse usually gets called next by a distant cousin who passes on the message to you. It's psychological warfare and your best option is to get on the phone with the collector and engage in the process.

Money owed is money owed and I respect the efforts even when I abhor the tactics. Unfortunately, a few collectors have turned nasty and personal, attacking the debtor for being trash, throwing other public failures in their faces, like a divorce, and really hitting below the belt: "your kids must be disgusted with you," and so on. Just ignore it.

Personal debt is much worse than corporate debt. Although a corporation can be wound down and dissolved, a person cannot. A business can have no future earning potential, but a person will have future earning potential, until they are dead. So, while a creditor might take a huge loss on a business liquidation, knowing the company will disappear and that this is their one and only chance to collect, a collector of personal debts might choose to hang out and wait a few years to collect from you later.

Now, of course, a collector isn't going to actually wait several years, they will call and mail you several times then sell your debt at a discount to the next guy. Collector 2 will take you through the same torturous collection process with all the threats and intimidation. If unsuccessful, he'll then sell your file to the next guy, at the next level of discount. Five years later someone will have your file, which has been accruing interest and debt, and they'll be working to shake you down as well. If a large enough sum, your file will eventually end up with a shady law firm who buys these debts for pennies on the dollar. They'll file suit in some far away jurisdiction, which you will then have to defend, or they'll get a default judgment and then they will seek to collect from you and place a lien on your assets. These law firms are not your typical well-dressed attorneys in a swanky downtown office; these are boiler rooms full of low-paid trolls making hundreds of dials per day while others mail letters and file motions in a vulture's symphony of debt collection. Their model may only need a 1% hit rate, but if they latch on to you, you may soon be spending tens of thousands of dollars in legal fees and settlements. There are books on the subject if you want to understand just how nasty personal debt collection can be.

Restructuring Unsecured Debts

You can restructure unsecured debts in many ways but generally the more effort and formality you build into the process, the better the results. Many entrepreneurs or their controllers/CFOs take the delay-and-pray approach and eventually deal with creditors one at a time, haphazardly. If the entrepreneur or CFO is a pleaser personality type, telling people what they want to hear, these debts will get resettled every few months forever, with zero credibility, and higher prices as the only result. Eventually, the business settles with some sort of monthly payment plan, but CEO credibility is shot, prices have increased, and the business will never fully recover.

When the company can reasonably afford to offer a settlement, a better approach is a simple letter explaining that the company has been challenged and needs to settle its debts in one of three ways: (1) discounted to induce a payment, (2) stretched out over a long payment period, or (3) pushed down or subordinated to a lower status. The following tactics work very well in smaller businesses, those under $50 million in revenues, because they have smaller vendor balances. The difference of restructuring the debts of a $10 million business versus a $100 million business is driven by the size of vendor balances. Most companies will restructure $25,000 in debt without a second thought but if the balance is $250,000 they're going to proceed much more cautiously, and probably with legal counsel.

The letter (see Figure 8.2), like all creditor letters, seeks to accomplish the following;

- Candor earns credibility, so accepting your debt in the first sentence is important.
- Strike a distinction that the business is viable (cash-flow or income statement) but the debt level is not viable (balance sheet).
- Softly remind the reader that they are low on the debt stack and have few options.
- Reinforce the bank's almighty power and how they must be appeased first.

Dear Valued Supplier,

As you know, ACME Manufacturing has fallen behind on our credit account with you. Unfortunately, you are not alone, because we've also gotten in trouble with debt to all our other suppliers plus our bank, the IRS, and our landlord. We have addressed the underlying issues with the business and are above breakeven again on our operating cash flow. Our bank and the IRS have supported us so far but we need to restructure our debts with them plus pay off some lingering regulatory fees.

To become sustainable, we need to restructure our unsecured vendor debts as well. We have gained permission from our secured creditors to make a one-time offer for settlement of unsecured debts. We are committed to paying you 100% back over time and have secured cash from a shareholder to offer a discounted alternative for quicker payment if that is more appealing to you. You can choose either and we will document your decision with a letter of consent or a letter of release. Creditors who choose not to participate in this limited offer will remain as general unsecured creditors of the insolvent ACME Manufacturing, with no clear path or ability to service these deeply subordinate debts.

For 37 long years ACME Manufacturing has been a strong part of our community and provided many good-paying jobs through our own business and those of our supplier partners. We're here because of you and our customers, and we appreciate your support through these trying months.

Please select between your past due balance of $_____ being paid:

    a. In full, 100% in equal monthly payments spread out over 10 years with payments starting in 24 months.

    b. One lump sum amount wired into your account at 20% of current value (an 80% discount) in 60 days.

Again, we appreciate your support. Please circle your choice above and return to us by (date, seven days later) in the enclosed self-addressed stamped envelope or digitally to limitedcreditoroffer@Acmemfg.

Sincerely yours,

John Smith – CEO

Figure 8.2 Formal restructuring letter.

- But, mention how the bank is being helpful and create a sense that everyone is helping support the company. Given the choice, most people are naturally inclined to follow the herd.

- If true, obliquely mention regulators. That always garners some sympathy or at least an appreciation for what the company is dealing with. If you have overdue tax payments, then mention that the IRS is being supportive and working with you. This reinforces where they are in the debt stack and how creditors are all being helpful through this process.

- Humbly cast the business (management) as having suffered great penance and retribution but also being now worthy and well positioned for a fresh start. Don't underestimate the creditor's lust for vengeance on the debtor; unsecureds will have this emotion as well.

- Management really wants to make you whole, but the math just doesn't support that hope.

- Use bankruptcy-specific language where you can, it provides credibility when your vendor's attorney reviews the letter.

- Isolate those who make poor decisions. No one wants to be in an "unfunded, unsecured, and subordinate group."

Despite all those emotional levers, we want to be quick and to the point in our letter. The situation is this, your options are A, B, or C, which is to do nothing and cut yourself out of the payment offering.

With a formal restructuring, you can segregate the general unsecured creditor class into two groups; those who took your generous offer and are now in the budgeted priority payment plan and those who didn't and are now unbudgeted and somewhere behind the priority payment plan. This means that the creditors who did not register their choice have been subordinated one significant level in the debt stack, beneath their former peers.

This simple letter works. Many creditors will chop their debt because they want to move on and support your business. Chances are they've already removed your aged payable from their collateral borrowing base and will properly write off your debt by end of year. If you get everything right with the mailing you can have a two-thirds rate of response, trending toward the smaller balances. It's a good way to clear the deck and help you regain control of accounts payable. Others will throw away your letter and seek to enforce collection on the entire amount. But as a creditor it's hard to imagine doing much better than what we've offered.

A more powerful letter will be similar to above but on letterhead from a leading regional bankruptcy/restructuring attorney. Creditors will likely pass your letter on to their attorney and having a powerhouse name signed at the bottom adds weight to your efforts.

The businesses liabilities after this effort might look like Figure 8.3, which saved you $700,000 on the surface but you also deeply subordinated another $300,000 and did a massive stretchout on the better part of $500,000. This doesn't change your balance sheet much but it cleans it up and respectfully deals with your unsecured obligations. Your vendors will accept this or not but it helps them get over it and move on.

Unsecured Restructure - ACME Mfg.		
		Restructured
Liabilities in Priority Rank	Book Value	Value
1st Bank Revolver	2,100	2,100
1st Bank Term Note	1,500	1,500
2nd Bank - Cash Advance Loan	250	250
State BDC Loan, no PG	100	100
Family Loan, secured	1,000	1,000
Accounts Payable 1	1,500	500
Accounts Payable 2		300
Total Liabilities	**6,450**	**5,750**
	Discount	700
	% Recovery	93%

Figure 8.3 Debt restructuring.

Advanced Tactics in Restructuring Unsecured Debts

I once settled a client's personally guaranteed $230,000 credit-card bill for 1% of what was owed. That's a trick that I still charge for. Credit cards can usually be settled for 50% with one long phone call if you say all the right things to the right people. Something I haven't tried personally but have witnessed is that debt seems to be forgiven more quickly for people in rehab or psychiatric institutions.

Restructuring Secured and Unsecured Debts

After time, the bank will want to move on. The workout team must move your file and there are only two options: (1) "back to the line," which means back to your old banker buddy with the good golf game or (2) off to a new bank. That new "bank" may be a wonderful capital partner for you or it may be a sketchy lender charging 20% interest and with an itchy trigger finger for liquidations. Again, based on probably centuries of tradition, banks are loath to discount debt to anyone. They may very well agree that your debt level is unsustainable and they may modify amortization periods or terms but they are not going to reduce the balance. If they did, word would get out and they would look like chumps to their shareholders and depositors. Just one loudmouth at the country club bragging about how he kneecapped Local Community Bank would cause tremendous harm to the bank's reputation. So, to get around that they will allow debt to be reduced in (generally) only one of three ways:

1. Liquidation and collection on personal guarantees. ("We squeezed every last drop.")

2. What's called "A and B Notes" or "Hope Notes." The A note is what your restructured business can reasonably afford, whereas the B note sits there on your books and theirs, but it is unserviced initially.

3. Letting you refinance out of the bank whereby they take a deficiency.

Because the bank has all the laws, facts, and leverage, they will only accept the best possible deal for them. They can attain that through a bankruptcy or a receivership so they're not going to take anything less voluntarily. As with a bankruptcy reorganization plan, a restructuring starts with future projections of business performance and the ability to service debt.

The following restructuring proposal is a global solution for dealing with many levels of debt in our ACME Manufacturing company. If you've already made unsecured creditor settlements you can include those or, if unaffordable, you can re-negotiate them as part of this global settlement. The proposal seeks to take near term cash pressure off the recovering business by stretching out payment terms, suspending others and haircutting those lower down the debt stack. Several key points are that First Bank's debt is restructured but it should have no impact on their balance sheet. In fact, based on the business turnaround success the bank's balance sheet may actually strengthen with less accruals and regulatory scrutiny.

Restructuring Proposal

ACME Manufacturing

Date

Based on the current financial situation at ACME Mfg. and the nascent recovery of positive cash flow, ACME seeks to restructure its debt on the following terms.

1. First Bank will recover its full current revolver balance of $2.1 million through the future cash flows of the company. To allow ACME a sustainable recovery, $500,000 of the revolver balance will be termed out on a 5-year note with a 10-year amortization. The remaining $1.6 million will be serviced as part of an ongoing and active revolver.

2. Based on recent appraisal, the remaining $1,500,000 term loan balance remains under-collateralized by $300,000. Acme will service the collateralized $1.2 million on a 5-year note with a 10-year amortization. The $300,000 will be held in a B-note with one balloon payment due in five years.

3. In 4 months, ACME will receive a $500,000 equity infusion from an outside investor to fund vital capex needs and to retire some existing secured debt. Of the $500,000, Second Bank will receive $150,000 as full payment of the existing $250,000 cash advance loan.

4. The State EDC loan will be restructured as a 20-year mortgage with a second position on all collateral with no payments in the first 24 months. The state EDC will support the continuation of the business as a stable employer in our community.

5. The family will receive no funds in this restructuring and will forgive its debts in exchange for releasee from a limited personal guarantee.

6. The unsecured creditors are mostly vendors who ACME wishes to work with in the future. They will receive up to a 50% recovery paid as a 10% premium on new purchases for up to the first 24 months. Remaining unsecured balances under the 50% will be paid off in equal payments between months 25 and 60.

7. The remaining $350,000 of equity infusion will be used as working capital in the business.

ACME Mfg. - Complete Debt Restructure		
Liabilities in Priority Rank	**Pre-Restructure**	**Post-Restructure**
1st Bank Revolver	2,100	1,600
1st Bank converted to term note		500
1st Bank Term A-Note	1,500	1,200
1st Bank B-Note		300
2nd Bank - Cash Advance Loan	250	150
State BDC Loan, no PG	100	100
Family Loan	1,000	-
Accounts Payable	1,500	750
Total Liabilities	**6,450**	**4,600**

Figure 8.4   Proposal.

Figure 8.4 illustrates how this restructuring would play out on the balance sheet. Although debt is reduced by $2 million, more importantly, it is also stretched out to reduce near-term cash pressures.

Gaining Support

As in bankruptcy, this restructuring will require an incredible amount of persuasion, competence, and credibility. These are some key strategies to keep in mind:

- Always be ready, willing, and able to push the company into a prepackaged Chapter 11. If your creditors clearly understand oblivion they will be willing to support a more productive option. Creditors fear bankruptcy for several reasons:

1. Significant cost, which leads to an erosion of recovery.

2. Possibly unknowable and uncontrollable costs.

3. Tarnish to the business brand and reputation, which would reduce chances of recovery.

4. Possible loss of control. Valid or not, people fear the court system.

5. Liquidation values. Don't be afraid to share your liquidation analysis. It will often stop a belligerent creditor in their tracks.

- You are doing God's work – you are preserving jobs and vitality in the community. Everyone else is being selfish and myopic, which is why you must prevail.

- A business must be fairly balanced between its four major constituencies: customers, vendors, employees, and owners.

These listed restructurings, both through bankruptcy and out of court, were achieved at a corporate level, meaning that personal guarantees with the bank were never called upon. The entrepreneur/CEO was never made to reach into his pocket to satisfy these obligation shortfalls. The bank has likely kept CEO pay in line with the market during the restructuring, because they have no problem with a good CEO making a good living.

Chapter 9

Strategic Exits

"Jeff, this division has been losing money for years and offers no strategic advantage to the parent company. We need you to visit and let us know how to shut it down as efficiently as possible," said the private equity chairman. I drove deep into central Pennsylvania to a rundown, tired, and well-past-its-prime metal widget factory. They didn't even produce their own widgets, they were a low-tier job shop for mostly automotive customers. The division had been starved for cash since the bankruptcy of its parent company 10 years prior. What happened since was pure financial mismanagement, and this scrappy little division was now having to beg customers to buy the input materials because they could not get basic requisitions funded from headquarters far away in Kansas. This was driving customers away, and sole-sourced parts were now getting shopped around. Blood was in the water.

Long story short, I liked the business and I thought it would be a perfect acquisition for a strategic buyer but a risky acquisition for a financial buyer. My liquidation plan would net about $10 million for creditors, which would be a fair recovery from this level of mismanagement and neglect. But all the jobs would get wiped out, the county would lose its biggest employer, the tax base would take a hit, and hundreds of families would struggle to recover in an already depressed region. If I did everything right, got lucky on valuations, and tidied up all loose ends, it would still be a soulless victory. The town, county, region would be permanently harmed, and if I drove through 20 years later, I'd feel I had played a part in the decline.

Like a house buyer, I thought the company had "nice bones"; the employees knew their stuff, and even though they had grown soft over the years, they sincerely wanted another chance at success. The equipment was falling apart, but they had a good range of capacity in an adequate building. There were a dozen things wrong with the business, but still they had good customers and a decent backlog of orders. In my opinion, if you have a backlog, you probably have a business. I liked the customer list, I liked the industry, and I saw low fruit everywhere in operations. In the hands of a good operator, this business would flourish, these folks would all keep their jobs, and I'd go out of my way to drive through this small town 20 years from now.

I called my client and persuaded him to let me try to sell the business. Remember the salvation process from Chapter 5? That's what we did starting at a distressed sale. Our downside scenario was shut down and liquidation for about $10 million, which would go straight to the bank as the parent company, was deep in debt. In 60 days we had three strong offers with deposits.

Offer 1: $15 million cash as going concern. Will strip out the equipment and move to another factory an hour away. Buyer owned by family with very strong balance sheet.

Offer 2: $28 million with about half cash and the other half paid over time or performance based. Keep factory in town with promises to grow it. Private equity buyer.

Offer 3: $30 million all cash, close in 60 days, keep the business local. Boom, done, finished.

Buyer 3 was the home-town favorite. They had an all-star management team of four owners, all life-long industry experts who had outgrown their current facility. Our factory was the perfect upgrade for them, and they would manage this business like it deserved to be managed.

Each bidder was willing to pay what is essentially goodwill, more than the market value of the assets. What they were paying for was going-concern value, the value of the money that flows through the assets. Even though that cash stream was negative, buyers saw value. The business was losing 4% per month, so about $3.2 million on $80 million in annual sales. That means if you put $100 into the company today, you'd get back 96 cents, over and over and over. No one in their right mind would pay for this business; it was like a banana on the shelf, past its prime and turning slightly more brown with each passing day.

So how did we sell the business for such a premium? We focused on key attributes and applied the pressure of a quick sale.

Key Attributes

- **Customer base.** Any customer who put up with buying input materials, late shipments, and lack of support as these customers had, is obviously sticky. If they hadn't left yet, why would they now? Aside from being sticky, many were blue-chip customers on blue-chip product platforms. Although you might otherwise spend 20 years trying to get a part on (for example) a Ford platform, this beaten-down little company had five parts on Ford's bestselling vehicle. This immediately makes the acquirer a critical vendor with the opportunity to grow the business from there. Even a profit-breakeven product gives you several years of contribution margin, a vendor number, a relationship, and the opportunity to bid on future business. Multiply that by a few other blue-chip customers and you can see the value we were trying to sell.

- **Customer concentration.** The largest customer represented 30% of company revenue, which is a concern. If they pull out, you're in big trouble. But combined with the similar-sized acquiring company, that concentration drops to 15% with all the benefits of a new blue-chip customer. The same was true of industry concentration, because the high bidder was similarly overconcentrated in the agricultural equipment market, so, again, the acquisition brought immediate value in diversifying customer and industry concentration risk.

- **Contribution margin.** Sure this orphaned division was unprofitable, but it still had an industry standard gross profit margin. When redundancies were squeezed out, much of that gross profit margin dropped straight to the bottom line allowing for significant economies of scale. The combined companies didn't need two receptionists, two CFOs, or two vice presidents of sales or maybe even duplicative engineering or quality or production.

- **Customer tools.** Again, we already had all the tooling needed to service this business. The engineering, sales effort, and tooling were all sunk costs. Using the Ford business as an example, not only were we already in, all the costs associated with getting in had been spent.

- **Backlog.** We had six months of sales on the books, committed with customer purchase orders. Managed properly, this was money in the bank for a new owner. Many of these parts had three or more years left in their product life cycle, which, again, gave the acquiring company a bright future.

- **Industry knowledge.** The high bidder was an expert in the agricultural market, not the auto industry, but with this acquisition they would inherit engineering and sales teams whose average auto market experience was over 15 years.

- **Years in business.** When you go to market with a brand or company that is 50 years old, it signifies financial strength and stability. Even if you recently picked it up in a distressed sale.

We ran a going-concern auction process for the business. Twenty-two potential buyers were contacted resulting in the three premium offers mentioned above. We made it clear that this was a classic divestiture and the seller was a sophisticated corporate seller. There would be a quick and fair process without the games or the emotions you might get with an entrepreneur seller. We prepared the marketing materials, represented the company fairly but optimistically, being very clear about both the rough past and the bright future. Figure 9.1 shows historical financial statements along with our pro forma projections.

Only the high bidding party put in the time and effort to really understand the costing and profitability buried in our order book. They reverse engineered parts, rebuilt and rebid

Pro Forma P&L		Seller	Buyer	Combined
	Net Sales	**80,000**	**90,000**	**170,000**
Cost of Sales				
Material		33,600	34,200	64,600
Labor		8,000	7,200	13,600
Secondary		5,600	5,400	10,200
Other Direct:		10,400	9,000	17,000
	Total Directs	**57,600**	**55,800**	**105,400**
	Gross Margin	**22,400**	**34,200**	**64,600**
		28.0%	38.0%	38.0%
Expense				–
Indirect Wages		7,200	8,100	13,770
Other Expense		18,400	19,800	38,200
	Total Expense	**25,600**	**27,900**	**51,970**
		32.0%	31.0%	30.6%
				–
	EBITDA	**(3,200)**	**6,300**	**12,630**
		−4.0%	7.0%	7.4%

Assumptions:
- COGS to standard of buyer based on based on improved purchasing, equipment and process. Proven through deep engineering and cost accounting studies
- 10% reduction in combined indirect wages through redundancies

Figure 9.1 Realized acquisition synergies.

bills of materials, blind quoted parts, and rescheduled equipment to find hidden profits and were willing to pay for them. This intensive due diligence and deep expertise allowed them to be the high bidder at a bargain price.

Today the factory is thriving under new ownership. They've retained existing customers, brought in new business, exceeded projections, and added jobs to the community, preserving the tax base and property values of this isolated little town.

Distressed Buyers

As that story illustrates, the buyers who show up when a business is tanking are usually a mix of industry insiders and specialist private investors. The industry folks will be a mix of cunning bargain shoppers and tire kickers, whereas anyone naïve enough to overpay will be scared off by the company's instability. In general, strategic buyers will pay more than the private investors, because there is true strategic value in the acquisitions. Successful financial buyers of distressed businesses use speed, certainty, and professionalism to win deals at lower prices than their strategic buying counterparts.

Sellers of distressed businesses are usually either large corporations who want to divest themselves of an unprofitable division or bank workout departments who are forcing the sale of a privately owned business. Both sellers are business professionals who know that value is declining by the day and they want a clean, quick exit. We recently sold a distressed plastic injection molding business and received three acceptable offers:

1. The first offer was from a well-heeled family-owned business that looked like an ideal strategic buyer but was located about 800 miles away. They wanted a three-month due diligence process and another three

months to close. They seemed capable of financing the transaction, but it was going to have a significant impact on the family's wealth. The process was being run by the founder's kid who was CFO and seemed determined to showcase his brilliance through the process. The business would likely relocate and wipe out the local jobs. Their bid was for 100% of the debt owed.

2. The second offer was from another family business with much deeper pockets and five recent and similar acquisitions in the plastic molding business. These were veterans in every aspect of the business and would be an ideal future owner. They wanted six weeks for due diligence and another two weeks to close. It was obvious that they were going to be both fair and excruciating through due diligence. It was uncertain if they would keep the business in its current location or consolidate it to another factory out of state. The bid was for 80% of the debt owed.

3. The third bidder was a wealthy industrialist who built his fortune buying highly distressed businesses and holding them for the long term. Appraisals were in place, and I'd already performed liquidation analysis for the owner and bank. The industrialist's bid was net forced liquidation value on the assets, which is about 50% of the total debt owed, but also the full amount of the senior secured debt. The buyer required three days of due diligence, another seven days to close, minimal reps or warrantees. That offer would get the bank paid in full without the uncertainty of an auction, preserve the jobs, keep a tenant in the entrepreneur's building, and keep the area's largest employer in business.

If you're the bank and all you care about is getting your money back, then option 3 gets you there very quickly and with minimal risk. The bank also knows there is an unemotional, professional, experienced, and serious buyer behind the offer, which is very appealing to bank officers and attorneys. If you're the owner, the bank is making it very clear what you should do, and the business is losing money by the day. Therefore, option 3 looks pretty good to you as well. In American insolvency, only creditors have a voice. Workers and communities are mute unless they are owed past due wages or taxes. Were they to have a voice, the certainty and track record of option 3 would likely make it their top choice. Customers would also vote for speed and certainty. Vendors would be split wanting payments for past due invoices but also wanting a business they can continue with. Option 2 offers a fair recovery but with a little less speed and certainty, Whereas option 1 offered neither. Bidder #2 ultimately won.

The universe of effective distressed buyers is small. Few investors have the requisite turnaround experience and legal knowledge to take on these train wrecks. Fewer can attract investment capital for these free-wheeling ventures, almost no one can move at the required speed, and even fewer yet have the stomach for an as-is, where-is purchase of a deeply insolvent business. Although most distressed purchases are asset sales, the gutsiest buyers will offer to buy all the stock of a company, no reps or warranties, sight unseen, that day, for $1, and then hope they can sort out whatever mess lies beneath.

Like selling anything, the key to selling a distressed business is to identify the likely buyers and then create an auction environment where they are bidding against each other. This is tougher in insolvency, but your limited time becomes your greatest point of leverage. We can run an extensive sales process with only two weeks between teaser, process letter, factory tours, and final binding offers. The tight deadline gets rid of tire kickers and grabs the attention of serious buyers – and serious buyers are very competitive once you have their attention. With a few distressed buyers circling the remains, I can often get a strategic buyer interested in high bidding to knock out a future competitor. "You know, Shirley, it sure would be a shame to see those distressed industrial buyers become a new competitor of yours when you can pick up all the soft assets and the gross margin contribution for still-well-below market value."

Peaceful Liquidation

Sometimes you can't save or sell the business, and there are still ways for the business owner to get out gracefully. I know a gentleman who owned a languishing business. The owner was about 70 years old and his partner had died several years earlier. The business was losing money. Foreign competitors took advantage of exchange rates to undercut his prices, and he saw no relief in sight. His positive equity funded these losses but that, too, was running thin. In the end, he chose to shut down the business. Employees got a fair severance and vendors were all paid in full. He liquidated the assets, paid the bank off, and went home to focus on his golf game and grandchildren. The employees and community lost out, but not every business is saveable.

Friendly Foreclosure

But what happens when the business lacks the equity to pay off its bills and can't find a buyer? We covered that a little bit in Chapter 5 with the recycling company. Let me paint a scenario: your business is losing money, there is no buyer interested, and the bank is underwater on your loan. Perhaps you have a chain of small print shops or record stores; your customers are mostly walk-ins and offer no strategic value to a buyer; you have no backlog, engineering, or tooling; and no one cares about your industry knowledge in a dying industry. You still want to fight, but you're down to your last nickel. And the bank – they are done. They'll take the write-off, cut ties with you, and move on. You've got one move left: pursue full-on crazy denial of reality or embrace a friendly foreclosure.

In a friendly foreclosure you allow the bank to take possession of the company's assets and, in exchange, they give you some relief. This is often the best prescription for everyone involved. We know that the bank holds all the cards. You can bleed away your last few dollars paying for lawyers to slow the bank's unrelenting march toward your assets – or you can deliver yourself for penance and get on with it. You agree to act responsibly, and they agree not to rip your limbs off. Seriously, that's about the gist of it. Everyone agrees that there will be a swift, prescriptive, and just cleansing of the debt with cooperation from all parties. It leaves more money in the business for creditors and less for attorneys and advisors.

I handled several friendly foreclosures in the aftermath of the 2008–2009 global recession, two of which were lumberyards. In the case of the first one, the third-generation business owner had simply failed to run the operation well but had been kept afloat through the housing bubble. The bank was aggressive; they wanted a full liquidation and didn't mind the owner suffering in the process. My focus was on the big assets, which included about 20 acres of lumberyard, hardware store, truss facility, and commercial cabinet shop. Every so often, the entrepreneur would mention the small rented kitchen showroom an hour away, but I largely ignored it. There was no asset value there to work with and the (poorly prepared) financial statements showed losses everywhere. I contacted all the likely strategic buyers, but this was at the bottom of the housing collapse and no one seemed interested.

We managed the going-out-of-business sale and scheduled the auction. The owner was going to come up short, and the bank was not yet willing to let him off the hook. During that time, I realized just how passionate the owner was about this distant custom-kitchen business. That was his true love, and he was really good at it. The lumberyard was just something he inherited from his family. With support of the bank, the entrepreneur strategically retreated to his custom kitchen business and paid off the remaining debt from there. Five years later, the bank was fully paid off, and the owner has a debt-free profitable business that he loves.

Another set of entrepreneurs tripled the size of their lumberyard, truss, and pallet business right at the crest of the housing boom. The huge new second location had delays and budget overruns, opening to dead silence about two months after the Lehman collapse in 2008. The bank was deeply underwater and the owners had no idea what to do next. We negotiated a friendly foreclosure, sold off the truss facility to a foreign buyer, managed a going-out-of-business sale for the big new store, and listed the building with a local commercial realtor. The bank wanted every penny possible, so we also negotiated a purchase agreement and operating lease on the original small store with the wealthy owner of another lumberyard. He would fund and operate that store for up to 60 days with the option to purchase it. After 30 days he pulled out, unwilling to go forward with the purchase. My clients moved back in and pretty much sat around waiting for the bank to take the store and send them home. That store was their passion, and for years they had serviced a small but loyal group of local builders and do-it-yourselfers. With support from the bank, we found a way for these guys to keep the original location and support a small mortgage with a big B-note mortgage behind it. Eight years later, they are still in business and settled up with the bank several years ago.

Other friendly foreclosures have given entrepreneurs a release from personal guarantees and a fresh start. We've bought a couple of businesses in which the talented but failed founder kept a sales- or engineering-focused executive role, commensurate pay, and healthy stock options in a restarted business with a cleaned-up balance sheet and a disciplined cost structure. It's a dignified and profitable fallback for the right entrepreneurs.

Government Collections

While a debtor is cleaning up debts with the banks, it's easy to lose site of everyone who is collecting. The bank will quickly pounce on you when results slip, but the federal government moves much more slowly, and it's easy to not see them gaining momentum. If you have an SBA-backed loan or owe taxes, it's the same friendly folks over at the U.S. Treasury that you'll have to deal with. Their mandate is to collect "the people's money" from you and return it to the Treasury.

The restructuring of IRS, SBA, and other federal debts is done through the offer in compromise, which is a structured administrative process of dealing with insolvent government debts. Like bankruptcy, it suspends collection actions and gives you time and cover to solve these issues. You will lay yourself bare and follow a formula. The federal government will be sizing you up by thoroughly, examining all your assets, and performing an audit of reasonable recovery potential. That's the baseline collection budget they feel you are worth. It's the sum value of all your assets sold off at auction plus a large portion of your future income for the next six years. If they believe they can just liquidate you to collect, why should the U.S. taxpayer accept one penny less? That's what you're up against. An IRS defense specialist, usually an Enrolled Agent, will help you build a case and get through it with the least amount of pain.

The government does want to collect what you owe, but they don't want to be unfair and they don't want to force you into poverty, so they have developed standards with the help of the Bureau of Labor Statistics and the Consumer Expenditure Survey. This means the U.S. government has determined what minimum amount of money you and your family need to meet your basic living expenses (as defined by them, not you). It's complicated, but here's a quick summary to give you an idea:

So a family of four can support itself on less than $55,000 annually. You might notice what's missing:

- Education or college savings

- A second or third car

IRS Monthly Allowable Expenses (2017)	One Person	Two Persons	Three Persons	Four Persons
Food	345	612	737	845
Housekeeping Supplies	32	65	66	65
Apparel and Services	83	138	193	293
Personal Products and Service	36	63	73	77
Miscellaneous	143	254	309	370
Housing and Utilities	1,436	1,686	1,777	1,981
OOP Health Care (<65 y/o)	49	98	147	196
Owning One Car	485	485	485	485
Operating One Car	250	250	250	250
Monthly Totals	2,859	3,651	4,037	4,562
Annualized Totals	**34,308**	**43,812**	**48,444**	**54,744**

Figure 9.2 IRS Monthly allowable expenses. (2017) Source: https://www.irs.gov/businesses/small-businesses-self-employed/national-standards-food-clothing-and-other-items.

- Vacations

- Yacht club

- Yacht

- Kids' sports programs

- Diapers, day care

- Holiday expenses

- Retirement savings

How's that for a debt stack? You get to subsist at government standards and they collect everything else. Don't like them apples? Shall I have the U.S. Marshal show you a worse option? These are the rules of the game. The good news is that this is as tight as you can be squeezed, and only for up to six years, after which there is a jubilee and you are released from your tax obligations, assuming you were not criminal in your actions, had good representation, and were compliant throughout. Either way, we are playing tackle here folks, and if you're willing to go into debt with government funds, you need to know the price of getting out.

When your back is up against the wall and the business is absolutely not going to survive with current ownership, there are solutions. They require as much speed and complexity as any other topic we've covered in this book but in the last weeks of a business, the potential value can still swing wildly, delivering the business owner any potential outcome between a great future and what will feel like federal debt slavery.

Chapter 10

Building Long-Term Value

If you've survived the gauntlet of the last nine chapters, made it out with your business, and didn't get wrapped around the wheel of some regulatory agency, well then, congratulations! You've just made it through the toughest obstacle course in business and you've now got a smooth-running, leaned-down business with an affordable balance sheet. You've also picked up a little scar tissue from the journey, but it looks good on you. Wear it with pride. As the thrill of the initial cash crisis and the grind of the turnaround both fade into memory, you've got a clean slate and a bright future. It's the first time in a long time that you've been able to take a full breath of fresh air and reflect on life.

You may be exhausted and simply wish to sell the business and move on. Or maybe your kids are now interested, or maybe you'd like to do an ESOP (Employee Stock Ownership Program) sale, or sell to your managers through an MBO (management buyout). Or, perhaps, you're enjoying the business again and really like the idea of holding it for the next 5–10 years. All these options and more are available to a well-run company with strong, predictable, and recurring profits, good management systems, and a strong balance sheet. Said another way, by maintaining your momentum coming out of a turnaround and being able to post 3+ years of strong, audited, earnings, then you really have every opportunity available to you as a business owner. What creates the most value for you in keeping the business also creates the most value for you in selling the business.

These are the four best things you can immediately do for your business:

1. Get rid of the turnaround consultant. He's a gun slinger and what your company needs now is a sheriff. Release the consultant back to the wild so you can focus on your own team and your own future.

2. Maintain a monastic focus on the fundamentals of running a lean and profitable company. Most importantly, stay scrappy even when times are good.

3. Gain core strength and accumulate resources. Become hard to kill, and let others take the big hits during the next recession.

4. Pick the right strategic direction now that you're lean and flexible.

The monastic return to fundamentals in recovery is often moving business management back into the ERP (computer enterprise resource planning system) and committing to be a process-driven organization. It's also committing to annual CPA audits and building all the financial and IT safeguards to help you sleep well at night.

Gaining strength includes regular preventative and predictive maintenance schedules for equipment, employee development, training, certifications, and re-entrenchment with your best customers. You're rebuilding the foundation of your company to make it recession proof. This is developing a lean culture and becoming process driven, which is an entirely different skillset than the firefighting nature of a turnaround.

Business Model

In Chapter 5 we covered ways to rethink your business model and become more cash and profit resilient. This might mean outsourcing your administrative functions or your sales efforts. It could mean retrofitting your product for new customers or moving into new markets as a natural hedge to your existing markets. You need to study your business, your industry, and adjacent businesses and industries that you know of. This is a good time to go slow. You're now the sharpest sword in our industry. What are you going to do with that? You don't have the balance sheet of the big boys but you're on our toes like no one else.

A review of your operational cycles can reshape your business in a way that quietly strengthens your balance sheet to the disadvantage of your competitors. For instance, parts used in the construction of nuclear power plants are big, expensive, and have "lumpy" demand, meaning that when a nuclear facility is being constructed, you have work and when there is no demand – you have no work. That's an awful business model. A better model is something with a steady pull demand; for example, bottled water. All day, every day people are buying and drinking bottled water, so there is very little "lumpiness" in orders. Bottled water has some seasonality to it, so maybe a vitamin company is a better model because people take their vitamins every day. You can set your production cycle to perfectly match that pull demand. The ideal operating cycle is probably a subscription-based business where people pay you in advance for their vitamins or digital news content.

Now you can't turn a massive steel fabrication facility into a vitamin company, but you can understand the weaknesses of your model and seek to improve it in creative ways. Lumpy revenue streams can be flattened with progress billings, different credit terms, prebuilding or inventory holds, using consigned materials, selling to a stocking distributor, selling to more and different markets. Fixed costs can be made more variable; with a reduction in overhead, using more contract labor, accrual arrangements with utility providers, revolving lines of credit, and so on. If you bend the demand and overhead levers far enough, you could end up with a business model that dramatically improves its ability to generate cash.

Governance

Statistically, private companies with an independent board of advisors do better than those without. Note that this is a board of advisors, not directors. You assemble the best people you can find, organize them into periodic meetings, and solicit their advice. In theory, they help you make better decisions and stay out of trouble. Certainly, managing a board will help the entrepreneur think, plan, and operate at a higher level. Our family business had four outside directors and three family members, and their advice often helped us make better decisions. All four outside directors were brilliant and hugely experienced; they had all run businesses much larger and more successful than ours.

At the time of my first turnaround, we had been hit with a dramatic market shift and were in a really poor position to react. I was active in an outside CEO peer group at the time, which met monthly. With all that support, our business still ended up in a very tough predicament. "Now is when you need us the most," said my CEO peer group. "No, before now was when I needed you the most. What I need now is time and money, neither of which I can afford for this group," was my response. Our board took a similar hiatus during our turnaround because none of them had that expertise. That being said, I still recommend a board of outside advisors for any private business not in crisis. The frequency and structure will help you work on your business instead of just in your business. The time to develop an agenda and presentations will help you step back from your business and think more deeply. It also provides a great opportunity to develop your staff.

People

Getting the right people in the right places is critical. In the early days of a turnaround, there are two documents that I have on hand at all times: my copy of that day's cash-flow forecast and a copy of that day's organization chart. I think the CEO has to obsess about the org chart as a sports team's general manager would, always trying to move or develop people in a way that best suits the team.

Training and development budgets are usually gutted in a turnaround, but they should be added back into the recovery budget. It's the reinvestment in your people and team that will help the company rebuild its balance sheet. Additionally, the company has already experienced the high cost of carrying too many people or the wrong people. All those layoffs you didn't think the business could withstand, they were handled just fine. This tough, leaned-down team will be your core going forward. They've been through a lot, so don't forget to share the fruits as your company recovers.

Sales

Think of yourself as the general manager of a pro sports team. If you're capped by league rules at 20 people, some managers will hire the best 20 people they can find, then spend all their time training, coaching, motivating, inspiring, incentivizing, and begging them to sell more. I used to do that and found it exhausting. What I found works much better is to recruit the best possible team at above-market wages, give clear directions, measure and rank them, then fire the bottom ranked person and upgrade the team with a new recruit. Your wages make recruiting a replacement pretty easy. Each time somebody leaves; rehuddle your team, give better training, better direction, then measure and fire the new bottom ranked person. Replace them and repeat, maybe quarterly. I think it's a perfectly fair trade; the company pays well, treats you with respect, offers a great opportunity, and will never ask you to carry the bottom ranked person with your hard work. The superstars will love it, the bottom ranked will avoid you, and the mass of them in the middle will be pulled toward the light.

I once hired a sales manager who immediately held a one-week sales contest; the top-three order writers would earn some amount of cash bonus. It worked fairly well for maybe half of the sellers, and the top five really hustled. The next week she held another contest in which the top three people to open new accounts would get some special recognition; a special parking space or trophy or something. Same thing, about half seemed motivated and a somewhat different top group really hustled. I was intrigued but far from impressed. I was paying her for strategy and long-term results, not a series of simple little promotions. When asked, she shared the brilliance behind her strategy: "There are only three types of sales people: the ones who are motivated by money, the ones who are motivated by recognition, and the ones who are motivated by something more complex than either of those. I'm a sales manager, not a psychologist, so in two weeks we know who is motivated by money, who is motivated by recognition, and who needs to be replaced by someone that is easier to motivate. If I have a team of easy-to-motivate sales people, I can accomplish great things with them, and that's what we're going to do." I walked away amazed and impressed.

Accounting

Coming out of restructuring, it is time to reestablish your rules for accounting. CPA annual audits are expensive and a lot of work, but nothing helps you sleep better at night than a squeaky-clean set of books. Every private-equity-owned company I work with has audited financials, whereas few entrepreneur-owned companies do. Any broker or investment banker will tell you that the cost of five years of audits is usually rewarded many times over in a sale because it gives the buyer great certainty in the business.

Now is the time to set guidelines with accounting and accrual policies, while also establishing proper controls to guard against embezzlement, fraud, or mistakes. Your CPA can help you with this.

The turnaround has probably focused you in on the important reports of the business. The other reports you can eliminate to reduce clutter and bring focus. For me, I just want to see upstream in the order cycle to our own sales and marketing efforts and downstream with rolling financial and cash-flow projections – no bells and whistles, just a clear view to each horizon.

Fraud Prevention

A banker friend once pointed out to me how many middle-aged bookkeepers are prosecuted for embezzlement. I've watched since then and it seems like several per year just in our sleepy little state, plus others I know that were not prosecuted. Embezzlement requires only weak financial controls from the entrepreneur and a lapse in honesty from the controller. It's my opinion that strong financial controls will deter even the most dark-hearted controller. The one thing you can count on is that everyone will watch how you respect and protect your money, and then they'll do less than that.

Larger CPA firms will provide process audits to help you set up the safest protocols for managing your treasury function. There needs to be a productive check-and-balance system in which activities are matched and authenticated before money leaves the building. They'll help you set up appropriate checks and balances for purchases, payments, payroll, and so on. Not only does it deter theft, it's the proper way to run your business. Sloppy accounting controls are like an unlocked door in a bad neighborhood; it's a dangerous temptation.

Culture of Theft; Culture of Free

Albany, the capital of New York, had a famous family-owned steak-house restaurant that was the meeting place for area big shots in business, law, and government. The owner was a gregarious guy who was always quick to buy a drink for the Governor or other high-profile guests. But he always pulled the cash out of his pocket to pay the bill. Always. His family paid for food and drinks, in cash, no exceptions. Years later he died, his sons took over, and they were more liberal with giving away drinks. The waitstaff saw this, and they became more liberal with drinks and food. The bartenders saw this, and they, too, became more generous with drinks and started skimming cash. Within a few short years the famous restaurant was out of business.

Years ago, an employee of ours was caught pretty much red-handed selling our stolen product. One of her boyfriends convinced her that loading up a trailer of our product (from our warehouse, on the weekend) and selling it on eBay was a foolproof way to make some extra cash. We found out and had the police visit her at her desk. She admitted everything; then we fired her and sought to press charges. The district attorney said we didn't have a case (years later this same Louisiana DA and his sheriff and our mayor are now all in prison on separate corruption issues). I was flabbergasted but slowly came to understand their (weak) point; because we had given away free product before to employees (always under $100 and for fundraising purposes to a local church group or sports benefit), we had set a precedent, and this employee was "confused" between a handful of product with permission and a trailer load without permission. Right or wrong, it drove home the points about consistency, documentation, and procedures.

Once I attended an industry event with an FBI agent in charge of prosecuting corporate fraud cases. He explained the moving target of FBI priorities; sometimes terrorism, some-times drugs or mortgage fraud, but rarely basic embezzlement in a small to midsized entrepreneurial company. The secret, he said, to getting an FBI agent to take interest in a pedestrian embezzlement case is to allow them to use their superpowers. "Think about it," he said, "we join the FBI so we can do all the cool superpower stuff like wiretaps, warrants, undercover work, etc. Bring me a lead that needs investigation services and I'm interested. Bring me a case that is all wrapped up like a Christmas present and there's nothing left for me to do. That's not nearly as interesting to me or my bosses."

Budget and Strategy

Strategy can be a really fancy and complicated subject if you let it. To me it's simply: what do you want to accomplish and how can you get there? Most entrepreneurs want to have a good life and a big payday when they exit the business. That may not be easy, but it does not have to be complicated. Here's an example of a family friend who has a furniture business that can produce approximately $10 million of furniture in a year. For 30 years he's maintained roughly that same $10 million revenue through all sorts of booms and busts in the business. For the same 30 years, he's been determined not to spend another dime on expanding capacity, but, instead, on maximizing the building and equipment that he owns. In good times, he raises prices enough to maximize profit. In tough times, he lowers prices to keep his crews and equipment running efficiently. He's moderated risk, eliminated debt, focused on quality, and made a great living as one of the few remaining U.S. furniture makers. You'll never get a high-priced consultant to suggest that strategy, but it's one of the best I've ever heard.

Contrary to what many creative entrepreneurs believe, strategy is the elimination of options. Every entrepreneur has dozens of opportunities, but strategy is set by the discipline to focus in on the one or two opportunities that make long-term sense for the business. The smartest entrepreneurs get into a business with their exit plan already mapped out. Of course, there are all sorts of surprises along the way, but these entrepreneurs know where they are headed and will get there eventually.

Profitability and Budgets

It's no great secret that running a business is all about profits. Everything else combined (multiplied even) means nothing without profitability. I've seen lauded CEOs end up on the pavement when their lucky streak ran dry and they didn't know how to do the tough work of squeezing profits from tough times. Another thing I've learned over the years is that losses are forever, whereas profits are only transient. It seems that a year of losses follows you forever, whereas a year of profits is immediately under attack by changing market conditions. The natural order of businesses is toward entropy, so every day you are defying those odds with the best thoughts and efforts you and your team can muster. The single best tool to ensure long-term survival is the humble budget.

Financial budgets are the one single activity most positively correlated with successful businesses because budgets make you think, reduce surprises, and give you visibility. I'm lumping management accounting and performance metrics in with budgeting because they are simply steps toward achieving the business's goal. For me it's like flying a plane; I'd rather have an instrument panel in case I end up in the clouds or the dark. The budget and all the supporting measures are just that, an instrument panel to help you operate the business. And even with that said, my guess is that more than half of businesses between $5 and $50 million in revenues do not have a formal budget process that gets reviewed monthly and that leads to management adjustments.

Financials

The trick here is knowing your numbers cold. There's really no excuse for not knowing the measurements of your business as well as you know your kids. Chances are your business is paying for their college tuition and their inheritance anyway. The best CFO I've ever worked with gave me estimated financials on the 29th of every month. By the 5th day, I had finals and we were presenting results to the bank on the 10th of every month. This was a highly leveraged manufacturing job shop with mostly Defense orders, so our volumes fluctuated wildly (a 300% swing between our high and our low months). But I always knew exactly where we were, and our banker called us the best reporting credit in his portfolio. I see no reason why every business can't run like this. If your controller can't get you there, it may be time for a new controller.

Receivables – be tough. You are not a bank. I know a company that will cut off the U.S. Department of Defense over late payments, and they don't budge. That's how confident they are in their products and service.

Clean Living

Intuitively, we all know the value of good habits in our lives and businesses. Avoid smoking, alcohol, and pork rinds. Exercise, stretch, and eat your vegetables if you want to be healthy. The same mentality works in business, and the very best companies embrace and leverage improvement programs like 5S and Lean. There is a certain magic that happens when you measure and run a tidy ship. Quality and on-time delivery improve, which sets off a wave of other positive effects: happier customers, more sales, pricing power, earnings, etc. No, I cannot draw a quantifiable linkage to these events, but I see the positive consequences of Lean and 5S everywhere they are well implemented.

Spend time building a personal relationship with your bank. Get to know everyone on the credit committee, and stay in touch with them through good times and bad. Attend their events and invite them for factory tours and management presentations. I have received calls from banks that have gone to great lengths to tell me how this troubled CEO is highly respected by the bank executives and they want to do everything possible to support the borrower through a tough patch.

Summary

If this was a book on boxing technique, you would now know exactly what to do when you step in the ring – and almost assuredly you would get beat up when you did. Although I can share the strategy and tactics of the turnaround game, what can't be taught in a book is the subtle artistry of the fight. When to bob, when to weave, when to just take the hits and when to attack. Boxers train daily and for years to hone their craft, and eventually they do more giving than receiving in the ring. Meanwhile, business owners or executives are more like mugging victims. They are not honed and trained like boxers, they are soft and distracted, dropping a trail of coins as they wander into bad neighborhoods.

And when it's over, most entrepreneurs will take all those lessons and make sure to never go near that neighborhood again. It's what I recommend; be really good at what you do and avoid trouble at all costs. That's a really safe way to steer clear of future turnarounds and all the heartache they cause.

Another option is to assume that the business world is full of bad neighborhoods and that the only security you can ever really have is in developing your street fighting skills. That takes reps, not reading. It takes getting out of your comfort zone and getting scraped up along the way.

I don't think successful entrepreneurs are the ones who make it out safely with a clean uniform. Instead, the successful entrepreneurs are the ones who thrive in the mayhem, who give as hard as they get, who protect those who need protection, and can welcome the day's tumult with a big smile.

Nothing endures but change.

Heraclitus

RESOURCES

American Bankruptcy Institute (ABI). www.ABI.org

Association of Insolvency and Restructuring Advisors (AIRA). www.AIRA.org

Certified Turnaround Professional (CTP) and Certified Turnaround Analyst (CTA). www.turnaround.org/certification

Commercial Finance Association (CFA). www.CFA.com

Turnaround Management Association (TMA). www .Turnaround.org

BIBLIOGRAPHY

Bibeault, Donald B. *Corporate Turnaround*. Beard Books, 1999.

Branch, Ben, and Hugh Ray. *Bankruptcy Investing: How to Profit from Distressed Companies*. Beard Books, 2007.

Burkett, Jim. *The Learned Disciplines of Management, How to Make the Right Things Happen*. Management Press, 2013.

Davis, Marvin. *Take No Prisoners*. AMACOM American Management Association, 2008.

Dunlap, Albert. *Mean Business: How I Save Bad Companies and Make Good Companies Great*. Crown Business, 1996.

Foster, Bob. *Be Your Own Turnaround Manager*. Two Harbors Press, 2008.

Fuhr, Elliot, and Dewey Imhoff. *Credit Executive's Guide to Business Restructuring*. CreateSpace Independent Publishing Platform, 2014.

Goldstein, Arnold, and Nicole Ofstein. *How to Settle with the IRS for Pennies on the Dollar*. Garrett Publishing, 1997.

Goldstein, Arnold S. *Turnaround*. Garret Publishing, 2007.

Guy, Bobby. *Distress to Success*. FreneticMarket Press, 2011.

Herbert, Fred. *Business Turnaround Blueprint*. 2017.

Hovatter, Debra Lee. *Bankruptcy Fundamentals for the Financial Services Industry: A Handbook for Non-Lawyers*. Alexandria, VA: American Bankruptcy Institute, 2007.

Katz, Lee N. *How Not to Hire a Guy Like Me*. Schroder Media LLC, 2013.

Kibel, Harvey R. *How to Turnaround a Financially Troubled Company*. Kibel, Green.1991.

Larabie, André. *Business Turnaround Methods: 120-Day Program to Restore Your Business*, 2010.

Levitt, Martin Jay. *Confessions of a Union Buster*. Crown Publishers, 1993.

Machiavelli, Niccolò. *The Prince*. Dover Publications, 1992.

Miller, Robert S. *The Turnaround Kid: What I Learned Rescuing America's Most Troubled Companies*. HarperCollins Publishers, 2008.

Moyer, Stephen. *Distressed Debt Analysis*. J. Ross Publishing, 2004.

Musashi, Miyamoto. *Book of Five Rings*. Trans. by Stephen Kaufman. Tuttle Publishing, 1994.

Papes, Bob. *Turnaround: Saving a Troubled Business*, Cypress Publishing Group, 2002.

Pate, Carter, and Harlan Platt. *The Phoenix Effect*. John Wiley & Sons, 2002.

Quinn, Regis. *Redesign to Turnaround Underperforming Small and Medium-Sized Businesses*. CreateSpace Independent Publishing Platform, 2014.

Salerno, Thomas, Jordan Kroop, and Craig Hansen. *The Executive Guide to Corporate Bankruptcy*. Beard Books, 2010.

Shein, James B. *Reversing the Slide*. Jossey-Bass, 2011.

Silver, David. *The Turnaround Survival Guide: Strategies for the Company in Crisis*. Dearborn Trade Publishing, 1992.

Steinman, Sandy. *The Small Business Turnaround Guide: Take Your Business from Troubled to Triumphant*. Morgan James Publishing, 2013.

Sutton, Gary. *The Six-Month Fix*. John Wiley & Sons, 2002.

United States Bankruptcy Code & Rules Booklet. 2018. LegalPub.com.

Whitney, John O. *Taking Charge*. Beard Books, 1999.

INDEX

Printed and bound by CPI Group (UK) Ltd, Croydon, CR0 4YY

16/04/2025

14658516-0003